Reading, Writing, and Rummy

More than 100 Card Games to develop language, social skills, number concepts, and problem solving strategies

Margie Golick, Ph.D.

Chief Psychologist,
McGill-Montreal Childrens Hospital Learning Centre

Pembroke Publishers Limited

Pembroke Publishers Limited
528 Hood Road
Markham Ontario L3R 3K9

Canadian Cataloguing in Publication Data

Golick, Margaret.
   Reading, writing and rummy

Includes index.
ISBN 0-921217-04-8

1. Educational games.   2. Cards,   I. Title.

LB1029.G3G64 1986   371.3   C86-093721-6

Printed and bound in Canada by Webcom Limited

0 9 8 7 6 5 4 3

I am sorry I have not learned to play at cards. It is very useful in life; it generates kindness and consolidates society.

Samuel Johnson

Acknowledgements

Special thanks are due to my son, Dan, the family magician, who enriched my repertoire of card magic. I am very grateful to friends, relatives, colleagues, graduate students, and children around the world who taught me some of their favourite games or played a few hands with me to help me refine the playing rules. Some of them are Jill Golick, Jody Golick, Peter Golick, Colin Bailey, Duncan Churches, Jason Cole, Julissa Cole, Luis Cole, Damien Donawa, Adriano Eliseu, Enid Engelhard, David Gunn, Daina Green, Meryl Green, Olga Guiducci, Myer Katz, Rose Katz, Paul Krawczuck, Terri Kontagiannis, Benoit LeNormand, Stephen Lemieux, Kirsten Lighfoot, Lois McCurdy, Nina Rabinovitch, Sylvia Riddell, Georgina Rayner, Ann Schleiper, Jane Shulman, Marianne Stein, Howard Stein, Janet Takefman and Linda Wasserman

Illustrator: Jane Churchill
Editor: Lou Pamenter
Typesetting: Jay Tee Graphics

TABLE OF CONTENTS

For Jamie

Introduction

Twelve years ago I wrote *Deal Me In!*, a book on teaching and learning with an ordinary deck of playing cards. When it was published it seemed like the end of a project. It turned out to be a beginning. I could not have predicted how much fun its publication would bring me. It led to invitations from all over Canada and the United States to give lectures and workshops on teaching through card games. I talked to elementary and high-school teachers, to teachers of pre-school and kindergarten, learning-disability professionals, to teachers of the deaf and the physically handicapped, at schools for the mentally retarded, and at conferences for mathematics teachers. I even played cards with a group of children on national New Zealand television. At home, in Montreal, I was invited by teachers and their pupils to Friday afternoon card parties.

Children, left to their own devices, play. Alone or in groups, they bring enormous vitality to their games, learned or invented. Children who seem apathetic or uninvolved in the school room, listless when confronted with household chores, become alert, animated, and enthusiastic over anything that can be construed as a game. What makes a game a game? Why can't a page of arithmetic be as compelling as a hand of Black Jack? In games, the rules are important and the competition is important, as are the camaraderie and the combined elements of skill and luck. Of course, this is true of school examinations. But games have the special quality of "playfulness". They are engaged in voluntarily, and players, even after a streak of bad luck, can start over with a clean slate.

Games are not just frivolities. Most are highly intellectual endeavours and have rules that players must learn. This involves more than just rote learning of an itemized list; it calls for building a mental representation of the game — an internal model that allows the would-be player to develop strategies for successful play. This means that the game-player must understand the objectives, evaluate his own strengths and weaknesses, and his opponents' characteristics, learn routine procedures and probabilities associated with the game, keep track of play, and make judicious decisions and long-range plans. There are no better vehicles to train children to remember, to order and classify information, to reason, to look for solutions to problems, to plan ahead, and to begin to empathize with other people. They think about their abilities and temperaments and how these can affect their decisions.

And while developing these abilities, which are fundamental to every academic, scientific, and even social endeavour, games can provide practice in hundreds of subskills children need in order to succeed in school. Playing games can lead to fast responses — visual, motor, or verbal; to facility with numbers; and to a richer, more precise vocabulary. All of that is true for the whole range of games, from Hopscotch to Hangman, from Parcheesie to PacMan.

I have made card games my personal crusade because of a fascination with playing cards themselves — their history, the varied forms they have taken depending on time and place, their infinite possibilities for play, and their appeal to both sexes, to all ages, and to all cultures. Further, they are accessible, easily transportable, and inexpensive.

I collect cards; I have hundreds of different decks. Some differ in size; some have different shapes. The European cards have different suit markings that retain the predecessors of our suits — cups, swords, sticks, and coins. Among the less conventional decks I own are one in Braille, one for the partially sighted (where, along with large numbers, every suit has a different colour), a deck that teaches sign language, and one that teaches musical notation. Added to these are dozens of conventional commercial decks, chosen for their interesting backs — the styles ranging from abstract designs to Inuit art.

Introducing card games as teaching tools always leads to a lively discussion of whether or not they have a place in schools, a discussion that teaches me a great deal about local customs and philosophies. A teacher in a rural Australian one-room school wrote of her enthusiasm for playing cards with her students, "I am now a convert, and have become thoroughly convinced, as you suggest, that much learning can be achieved." She goes on to talk about cards' usefulness in developing skill in the fingers of poor writers and in developing math concepts in five-year-olds, and she concludes, "Perhaps more important than the skills learned are the values learned — sharing, waiting, taking turns, and learning to lose."

The sources for the games that follow are varied. They come from colleagues and from teachers, but mostly they come from children. In the Learning Centre where I work, children with learning disabilities come for help. We try to figure out what makes reading or math hard for them and teach them new ways of tackling their school subjects. I use card games as part of the assessment process, and I usually learn a game or two in the process, even from very reluctant clients. Not only do we evaluate children's strengths and weaknesses in the Centre, but we teach them. Cards are invaluable as an adjunct to a remedial session. When we take a game-playing break, I like to choose a game that will give practice in a skill we want to develop. On occasion I invent a game, but more often I modify an existing one so that it fills the necessary pedagogical role.

I have received many letters from teachers with some of their favourite card games or their variations on the games about which I have written. Many of them told of their experiences with cards as a teaching tool (including confrontations with parents or principals who disapproved) and what a useful aid cards had become to their classes in math, in their language-arts programs, or in sessions to improve finger dexterity.

Needless to say, those letters have given me enormous pleasure — and lots of new ideas. Best of all, I have had fan mail from children:

> Dear Mrs Golich
>   My favorite Card game
> is May I. I will like you
> to send a new games of card
> becauses we a sich of then thank
> youvermuch
>
>   Sincerely
>   Robbie

It is for Robbie that I am offering these new games and some variations on some old ones.

CARDS AS EDUCATIONAL TOOLS

Apart from the games and card tricks that can amuse and entertain, while providing educational side-effects, parents and teachers can use a deck of cards as the focus of innumerable activities that are more obviously tied in with educational objectives: to develop remedial activities for children and adolescents to enhance their language, reading, and math. The aim is to get them to look, listen, and read with precision, to practise computation, to develop orderly work habits, and to discover their own capacity to solve problems.

LANGUAGE PROBLEMS

We know that language difficulties — sometimes very subtle ones — are often the underlying causes of school failure. Children whose language is not as well developed as that of their classmates find it hard to put their ideas into words. They have trouble following directions and explanations in the classroom. It takes them longer to memorize verbal material — letter names, capital cities, dates, number facts. They may need extra time to learn how to read. When they finally master the mechanics of reading, they may have trouble understanding the vocabulary and the syntax of the books at their grade level.

Parents and teachers want to know if the language delay is cause for concern and if it is symptomatic of more general delayed development. Most of all, they want guidelines for accelerating the language learning.

Language problems can have a number of causes. In a child whose native language is not English, the apparent delay may be a result of poor language models or insufficient opportunity for learning. Delayed language can be the result of a hearing loss or, in a child with normal hearing, the result of hard-to-detect problems in processing, that is, registering and remembering, spoken language. Whatever the problem, it is important to specify it so that parents and teachers can understand what it is a child can or cannot do with language; then they can tailor language they direct to the child, and take appropriate remedial measures to stimulate the lagging areas.

The first step in language assessment — formal or informal — is eliciting a language sample. This is not always an easy task, particularly with youngsters who are shy or self-conscious and reluctant to expose their difficulties. They are apt to answer questions in monosyllables and resist embarking on any narratives or prolonged descriptions. For many years I have used card games to get children to talk. When children explain a card game to a would-be player, they have to maximize all their verbal skills. Teaching a game calls for considerable precision of speech. In the course of trying to teach a game to another player many children with language disabilities reveal the extent of their difficulties. In these situations it is easy to spot their word-finding difficulties, their inability to keep track of their own sentences, and their problems in organizing the ideas in an orderly fashion.

I have used cards, too, in informal investigations of children's comprehension. When children have trouble following directions I try to determine whether it is the length of the sentence that trips them up, or whether they have difficulty when there are directions or too many details that must be attended to, or whether there are some aspects of vocabulary or syntax that have not yet been learned.*

To that end I might lay out four or five cards, say a 4 of clubs, 4 of hearts, 2 of spades, 2 of diamonds, 5 of diamonds, and give several sets of directions to see how well they were understood. These could vary in difficulty depending on the age and ability of the child and what I want to find out. For example:

1. Put a red card on a black card.
2. Put a black 2 under a red 4.
3. If there is a black 5, put a black 2 beside it.
4. Put a 4 between two red cards.
5. Put a 4 to the left of a 5.

I might even prepare a set of written questions to explore ability to understand and answer in writing, questions involving simple

* A formal test of language function that uses pictures of playing cards as stimuli is the CELF Advanced Screening Test: *Clinical Evaluation of Language Functions,* E.M. Semel and E.H. Wiig, Charles E. Merrill, 1980.

numerical and spatial concepts. For example, questions for the array described might be:

1. How many cards are there?
2. Are there more blacks than reds?
3. How many different numbers are there?
4. How many even numbers?
5. How many odd ones?
6. Are there more 4's than 5's?
7. Are there more 2's than 4's?
8. What card is second from the left?
9. What card is left of the 2 of diamonds?
10. Is the highest card a club?

READING ACTIVITIES

Beginning readers need to practise their reading skill. This is true for six- and seven-year-olds whose reading is developing normally and for older children with reading disabilities who, even with suitable help, are learning slowly. A problem, particularly for the older children, is finding suitable texts. Primers or books written for beginning readers are usually boring and repetitive and apt to insult their dignity. Books for older children have vocabulary that is too wide-ranging, syntax that is too complicated, and sentences that are too long. Furthermore, they offer too little opportunity to rely on context to augment phonic skills that are just emerging. Artificial texts developed with limited vocabulary ("The cat sat on the mat") offer only the satisfaction of successfully decoding, but nothing for the mind — no new information, no suspense, no stirring of emotion, and no problem to be solved.

I am convinced that, in order for children to get hooked on reading, they need to know it as a vehicle for a mental challenge. I have found that a puzzle can be most useful and well-received. With a challenge — a problem to be solved — the reading is only a means to an end. Reading practice is incidental and is a source of satisfaction — not drudgery.

The puzzles I like usually involve some manipulation of objects, a necessity for reading the clues accurately, for following directions precisely, and a chance for logical deduction. I often build my puzzles around playing cards. Texts about cards have several advantages. They seem more frivolous to the child who may already be bogged down with too much "serious" homework; there is a finite predictable vocabulary (e.g. number words, names of suits); and there is plenty of opportunity to include important spatial, quantitative, and linguistic concepts. These tasks are good for developing reading comprehension. Reading comprehension difficulties come from inaccurate reading (failing to note the word "not" in a sentence), misreading a word ("chicken" for "children"), misunderstanding the meaning of a single word, failing to understand a particular sentence structure, or simply not registering or remembering part of the information conveyed.

In "puzzle" texts the reading is a means to an end. The solution depends not only on accurate reading ("decoding"), but on understanding concepts, remembering them, and following directions precisely. The readers always have immediate feedback that lets them know if their reading is correct.

Reminder: There is no limit to the number and variety of texts that can be made using playing cards as props. The following list is a reminder of useful words to be included in activities that will stimulate awareness of directional, spatial, and numerical concepts.

beside	second
below	third
above	fourth, etc.
next to	last
to the left of	highest
to the right of	lowest
underneath	second highest/lowest
between	some
nearest	all
farthest (furthest)	any
black	less than
red	more than
odd	if there is . . . then . . .
even	not (a card that is *not* red)
first	

Here are some sample directions that might be used as guidelines for parents and teachers who make up playing-card activities:

1. Put a red card between two black ones.
2. Put an even-numbered card next to the highest card.
3. If there is a black card, put a 10 next to a 9.

15

4. Put the 7 of spades to the right of the 7 of clubs.
5. Turn over any two red cards.
6. Pick up all the black cards with numbers less than 7.

The following are samples of puzzles that can be used as tools for stimulating language, reading, spatial awareness, and facility with numbers. With a deck of cards there are unlimited possibilities for creating your own.

Hit The Deck

From a deck of cards remove the jack of hearts, jack of clubs, six of clubs, six of hearts, ten of diamonds, ten of clubs, king of hearts, king of clubs.
Make two rows of four cards like this:

In the top row put a red king on the left.
Next to the red king put a black ten.
At the end of the row put a red ten.
Put a black six between the tens.

To make the second row:
Put a six under the black ten.
Put a black jack under the black six.
Put a red jack next to the black jack.
Put the king in the spot on the left.

Answer these questions:

How many kings in the top row?
How many tens?
How many sixes?
How many clubs?
How many jacks in the bottom row?
How many sixes?
Is a jack under a six?
Is a six under a ten?
Is a king above a king?
Is a red six between a king and a jack?

16

Figure It Out

The child is presented with four face-down cards (see below) and these clues:

1. The cards at the ends of the row are black.
2. A 9 is between a 7 and a 10.
3. There are two 7's.
4. The 10 of diamonds is directly to the right of the 9 of hearts.
5. The fourth card is a club.

Name the cards in order.

Turn over the four cards. Were you right?

Answer: seven of spades, nine of hearts, ten of diamonds, seven of clubs.

Rearrangement

Use the following directions with the same card arrangement as in *"Figure It Out"*, but display the cards face-up.

1. Take the last card in the row and put it between two odd-numbered cards.
2. Take the card that is now third in the row and put it in the leftmost position.
3. Put a card with an even number between two black cards.

What is the final order of the cards?

Answer: nine of hearts, seven of spades, ten of diamonds, seven of clubs.

Orderly Arrangements

Take all the cards from one suit.

1. Put them in numerical order (count jacks as 11, queens as 12, kings as 13).
2. Put them in alphabetical order. When they are in alphabetical order, is any card in the same position as it was in numerical order?
3. Add them up.

Which One Doesn't Belong?

Arrange cards as follows and decide, for each group, which one doesn't belong.

3♥ 4♥ 3♣ 3♦
5♥ 6♠ 6♦ 7♥
9♦ 10♥ 6♣ Q♣
Q♣ J♣ 10♣ K♣
Q♠ K♠ A♦ 10♠
9♠ 8♥ 7♣ 3♦
J♠ Q♥ K♥ K♠
2♥ 3♣ 5♠ 2♦

Follow Directions

1. Take out all the cards in one suit from ace to 10. Arrange them in two horizontal rows of five cards each as follows: a) every card in the top row is one more than the card directly below it in the bottom row; b) the numerical difference between the first and last cards in each row is eight; and c) the difference between the second and fourth card in each row is 4.

Answer: 2 4 6 8 10
     1 3 5 7 9

2. Take the ace (1), 4, 6 of hearts, the 7 and queen of clubs, and the 6, 8, 10 of spades. Arrange them in two rows as follows:
Put the face card between a red odd-numbered card on the left and a black even-numbered card above 9 on the right. To the right of the even-numbered card put a card of the same suit. Under the left-most card put a card that has a numerical value of six more than that card. To the right of that, put a red card that will be one less in numerical value than the card to its left. Make the card that is fourth from the left the same denomination (number) as the card that is second from the left. Put the last card in the remaining space.

Questions:

What card is below the ace?
What card is above the black 6?

Is the 8 in the top row or the bottom row?
What card is between two 6's?
Is the queen below a 5?
Is there an odd-numbered card in the bottom row?
What card is second from the right in the top row?
Is there a card between two red cards?

3. Take out all the red cards from a deck. Remove the face cards. Keep the rest of the deck handy.

   Arrange the hearts in numerical order in two rows of five cards each. Arrange the diamonds below them in the same way, so that there are four rows of cards.

   Turn over the left-most card in the second row from the bottom.

   Turn over the middle card in the top row.

   Turn over the last card on the right in the second row.

   Turn over the card next to it on the same line.

   In the bottom row take the first and last cards and trade places.

   Find a 5 above a 6 and turn over the card that is to the left of that 5.

   If there is a row with only three adjacent face-up cards, turn over the middle card of the three.

   Remove the last card of the second row from the bottom and replace it with a spade of the same denomination.

   If there is a vertical column with two 5's of the same colour, turn over the bottom card.

   Turn over a 7.

   Find a column that adds up to seventeen. Turn over the top card in the column.

   Find a row that adds up to more than thirty. Turn over one card so that the row will total twenty-four.

   Without looking write down the cards in the spaces:

—	2	—	4	5
6	—	8	—	—
—	2	3	—	5
10	—	8	—	6

Answer:
   First row: Ace of hearts, three of hearts
   Second row: seven of hearts, nine of hearts, ten of hearts
   Third row: Ace of diamonds, four of diamonds
   Fourth row: seven of diamonds, nine of diamonds

Questions (for the face-up cards):
1. What row has three even cards?
2. What row has two odd and one even card?
3. In what row do two of the three cards add up to the third?
4. The middle column has two cards of the same denomination. What are they?

Answer: 1. the fourth
2. the third
3. the third
4. eight of hearts, eight of diamonds

Listening For The Clues

A listening activity (or reading activity) can be constructed around the face cards that will give practice in careful listening (or reading), in looking with precision, and in systematic elimination of alternatives. To come up with the correct answer, players must delay responding until they hear the final clue.

Players should spread out the twelve face cards and, with each clue, remove the cards that are no longer candidates.

The following are sample clues that work with a deck produced by the International Playing Card Company, Ltd. (Windsor, Canada). Since court cards can differ, you may need to make your own set of clues. Encourage children to create sets of clues for each other. Part of what they will learn is how to create good clues that don't tell too much at once, but at the same time narrow down the possibilities.

I'm thinking of one of the face cards
It's male
It has a moustache
It does not have a beard
It's not red   Jack of spades

I'm thinking of one of the face cards
The figure is in profile
It is not a king
It is looking toward the suit symbol   Jack of hearts

I'm thinking of one of the face cards
It is not in profile
It is not red
It is female
She is facing left (her left)   Queen of spades

I am thinking of one of the face cards
It is red
The figure is holding something in the left hand
It is not a flower
It is held behind the head   King of hearts

I am thinking of one of the face cards
The figure holds a sword
It is not behind his head
He is looking toward it   King of spades

I am thinking of a jack
He is not looking in the same direction
as the queen and king of the same suit   Jack of clubs

Silly Sentences

Take jack, queen, king, ace of a suit. Shuffle them. Lay them out from left to right. See how many four-word sentences you can make with words starting with the first letters of each of the cards in order from left to right.

Samples:

King	Jack	Ace	Queen
Kangaroos	jump	around	Queensland.
Kermit	just	acts	queerly.
Ace	Jack	King	Queen
A	jump	killed	Quentin.
All	jewellers	know	quality.
Ace	Jack	Queen	King
Arthur	just	quit	kissing.
All	judges	quote	Kipling.

King	Queen	Ace	Jack
Kids	question	adults'	judgment.
Kinfolk	quibble	and	joke.

Jack	King	Queen	Ace
Just	keep	quiet	Ann.
Juggling	knives	quiets	alligators.

Variation: Take jack, queen, king, and ace of one suit. Arrange them in order from left to right in as many different orders as possible. Make a four-word sentence for each arrangement, with words starting with the first letter of each of the cards from left to right.

Can students tell in advance how many different orders there will be?

Samples:

A K Q J	A knight quit jousting.
A Q K J	All qualified kangaroos jump.
A Q J K	Authentic quince juice kills.
A K J Q	Americans know Japanese quotations.
A J Q K	A job quiets Kelly.
A J K Q	Aunt Judy keeps quiet.
K A Q J	Kumquats are quite juicy.
K A J Q	Keep all jokers quiet.
K Q A J	Keith quotes a journalist.
K Q J A	"Know quality", Joe advises.
K J A Q	Katherine joined a quest.
K J Q A	Kermit just quit answering.
Q K A J	Quentin keeps a journal.
Q K J A	Quit kicking Junior around.
Q J K A	Quebeckers just keep arguing.
Q J A K	Quakers just aren't kissers.
Q A J K	Quakes around January kill.
Q A K J	Quintuplets are killing jellyfish.
J A Q K	Jump around quickly, kids.
J A K Q	Jim always keeps quadrupeds.
J Q A K	Jeremy's quips are kind.
J Q K A	Jill quietly knits afghans.
J K A Q	John's knees are queer.
J K Q A	Judges keep quarters around.

These sentences were composed with a rule forbidding the use of the

22

actual words "king", "queen", "jack", or "ace". An easier version could permit them.

NUMBER CONCEPTS

Arithmetic skill requires practice — opportunities to play with numbers, manipulate them, and think about them. Activities with cards make this kind of play attractive to children and adolescents. But arithmetic involves more than just facility with numbers. To solve mathematical problems presented in words, calls on special skills — disentangling complex sentences, keeping track of several variables, pursuing a complicated thought, and, above all mathematicians tell us — actually visualizing the problem. Logical puzzles develop these skills. The following activities and puzzles will stimulate facility with numbers and mathematical reasoning.

Hat Trick

Challenger announces that he will give each player a card. Players are not to look at it, but to place it face-out on their forehead, so that it is visible to the other players. Challenger tells players that there will be at least one red card.

Challenger actually gives *three* red cards.

The first player to announce correctly the colour of his card is the winner.

This becomes an interesting activity when performed in front of a class and the players and audience consider the thought processes of the successful player. Something like this must take place:

Player A thinks: I see two red cards. If mine is black, then Player B will see red and black, and think, "If mine is black then Player C will see two blacks and know he must have red, and say so. He's not saying so, so mine must be red."

Player A notes that Player B is not coming to any conclusions, so he knows that he has red.

Challenge I

Pick out three cards and place them side by side to make a three-digit number divisible by eleven.

Solution: The two cards at either end must equal the middle card, e.g., 484, 693, 792, 121, 891.

Challenge II

Take a suit of cards ace through 10.
Make two lines each with five numbers that have the same total.

Challenge III

Take a suit of cards ace through 9.
Make three rows so that cards in each row have the same total.

Table-Top Tables

This novel way of rehearsing the multiplication tables helps to highlight and clarify what happens in multiplication. When the cards are laid out the child can see six 7's and understand what is meant by the notation 6×7.

Take three decks of cards. Remove the face cards.

Use the cards to construct multiplication tables (from 1×1 to 10×10). For example, to represent the six-times table, arrange in rows, on a large table (or on the floor)

    6 aces
    6 2's
    6 3's
    6 4's, etc., up to 6 10's

Then write the equations: $6 \times 1 =$ and $6 \times 2 =$ and fill in the answers.

If player does not know the answer, he can figure it out by counting the spots on the cards in each row.

Making Diagrams

1. Take the ace, 2, 3, 4, and 5 of diamonds. Place them on an imaginary diagram like this:

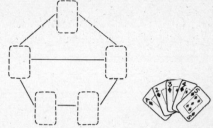

   so that no card is connected directly to an adjacent number.

2. Can it be done with six cards and the following diagram?

Answers: 1.   2.

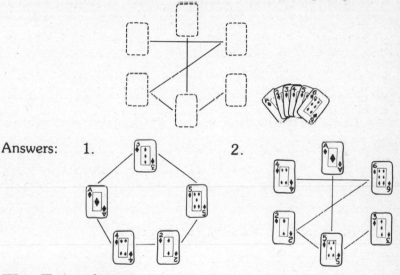

The Four Aces

The four aces are in a row. Try, from the following description of the layout, to answer the question.

The ace of spades is next to the ace of clubs, but is not next to the ace of hearts. The ace of hearts is not next to the ace of diamonds. What card must be next to the ace of diamonds?

Answer: ace of spades

Three's And Four's

Visualize three playing cards adjacent to one another (side by side). Listen to the following information and name the three cards in order from left to right.

1. A 4 is just to the right of a 3.
2. A 4 is just to the left of a 4.
3. There is a diamond just to the left of a heart.
4. There is a diamond just to the right of a diamond.

Answer: three of diamonds, four of diamonds, four of hearts

Replacement

Value of cards: Each club = 1, diamond = 2, heart = 3, spade = 4.

For each variation of "Replacement" read all the instructions before laying out the cards and try to answer the questions that follow before you carry out the instructions. Then lay out the cards as directed, answer the questions you couldn't answer, and check the answers you gave.

I. Instructions:
   1. Lay out twelve clubs in a row.
   2. Pick up every second card and replace it with a diamond.
   3. Pick up every third card and replace it with a heart.
   4. Pick up every fourth card and replace it with a spade.

   Questions:
   1. What is the total value of cards after each layout?
   2. After the fourth layout will there be more black cards or red cards?
   3. Will there be more clubs or spades?
   4. Will there be more hearts or diamonds?

II. Instructions:
   1. Lay out twelve hearts.
   2. Pick up every second card and replace it with a spade.

3. Pick up every third card and replace it with a club.
4. Pick up every fourth card and replace it with a diamond.

Answer questions from I.

Variation: To add to the challenge — if the questions cannot be answered without actually laying out the cards, try laying out the cards face down and try to answer the questions.

Then check the answers by doing it again with cards face up.

DIVERGENT THINKING

The nature of divergent thinking is the widening of perspective and the encouraging of more and more possibilities. Puzzles such as this one produce divergent thinking.

Making Sentences

Take four aces, each of a different suit. Shuffle them. Lay them out from left to right. See how many four-word sentences you can make with words starting with the first letters of the suits in order from left to right, such as the following:

Clubs/Hearts/Diamonds/Spades
Can hogs dig swiftly?
Chinese has different symbols.
Cold horses don't shiver.

Diamonds/Spades/Clubs/Hearts
Dead snakes can't hurt.
Dancers should come home.
Don't smoke cigarettes here.

Spades/Hearts/Diamonds/Clubs
Sam has dirty socks.
Shoes hurt Dad's corns.
Small houses don't collapse.

Hearts/Spades/Diamonds/Clubs
Have some delicious candy.
He should drink cocoa.
Heaven sent down chimpanzees.

Diamonds/Spades/Hearts/Clubs
Dogs should have collars.
Don't stay here, children.
Dieters shun hard candies.

Clubs/Diamonds/Spades/Hearts
Computers do something horrible.
Collect dry socks here.
Cats don't seem happy.

CLASSIFICATION OF GAMES

I have classified the games in this book under three headings: Games For Different Occasions, Games That Develop Particular Skills, and Games That Teach By Using The Characteristics Of A Playing Card. Some of the games and tricks appear in several classifications.

GAMES FOR DIFFERENT OCCASIONS

Good Games For Two

Ace Frimé
Add And Subtract
Back Alley Bridge
Briscola
Coffee Pot
Durak
Hockey
King's Corner
Knuckles
Odds And Evens
Odds Or Evens
Paul's Game
Places
Scopa
Xeri

For Varied Ages And Abilities

Ace Frimé
Big Bango
In Between
Jane's Grandmother's Solitaire
King
King's Market
New Market
Piri Picciu
Ronda Robada
Sentence Rummy
Speed

Fast Visual Or Verbal Responses

Asa Pilia Tutto
Bichos
Speed

For Very Young Children
Asa Pilia Tutto
Bichos
Big Bango
Burro Empé
Ciao Seppe
Donkey
Jackass
Jacks Wild
King's Market
Mariage
New Market
Paul's Game
Ronda Robada
Turkish Delight
Spoof
Suck The Well
Switch

Games Of Skill
Bichos
Burro Empé
Coffee Pot
Four In A Row
Nine-Five-Two
Nine to Zero
Three-In-A-Row For Four

Combining Luck and Skill
Durak
Fallout
Hit The Mark
In Between
Multiplication Rummy
Speed
Spoof

Games For Large Groups
Alliteration
Bichos
Big Bango
Dammit
Frustration
Gimme
Happy Birthday
Sentence Rummy

Games With Complicated Rules
All Fours
Bezique
Black Maria
Creights
King
Nine-Five-Two
One Hundred And Fifty
Turnover Totals

Easy To Handle
Add And Subtract
Bichos
Big Bango
Hit the Mark
Jackblack
Nines
Ninety-Nine
Odds And Evens
Paul's Game
Piri Picciu
Ronda Robada
Seven-Up
Three Card Indian Poker
Turnover Totals

Games Of Chance

Big Bango
Hockey
Jackass
Jacks Wild
Kajung
King's Market
Mariage
Myer's Solitaire
New Market
Odds Or Evens
Suck The Well
Switch
Xeri

GAMES THAT DEVELOP PARTICULAR SKILLS

Ordering

Airplane Solitaire
All's Well That Ends Well
Calendar Solitaire
Children Don't Have Secrets
Copy Cat
Dealer's Choice
Duncan's Trick
Five And Dime
Happy Birthday
Jack-Ass Ate Seven Trees
Janet's Challenge
Kajung
King's Market
Magic Fingers
Middle Of The Road
Myer's Solitaire
New Market
Over-Under
Pick A Card

Places
Poker Patience
Quadrille
Queen Bee
Seven-Up
Spoof

Visual-Spatial Concepts

Add It Up First
As The Ox Ploughs
Creights
Family Reunion
Over-Under
Queens On Top
Quadrille

Number Concepts And Computation

Ace Frimé
Add And Subtract
Add It Up First
All Fours
Airplane Factors
Airplane Solitaire
Black Maria
Briscola
Children Don't Have Secrets
Creights
Crossnumber Puzzle
Durak
Fallout
Fifty-Two Minus X
Finders Keepers
Four-Leaf Clover
Gimme
Guts
Hit The Mark
Hold 'Em
In Between
Jackblack
Jailbird's Trick
Jane's Grandmother's Solitaire
Jokers Out
Kajung
King
King's Market
Knuckles
Mark's Place
Multiplication Rummy
New Market
Nine-Five-Two
Nine to Zero
Nines
Ninety-Nine
Odds Or Evens
Odds And Evens
One Hundred And Fifty

Places
Plus Or Minus One
Piri Picciu
Ronda Robada
Royal Square
Scope
Seven And A Half
Seven-Up
Sevens
Speed
Spoof
Suck The Well
Thirty-One
Three-Card Brag
Three-Card Indian Poker
Tower of Hanoi
Turnover Totals
Witch's Brew
X Marks The Spot
X-Ray Vision
Xeri
Zero

Challenging And Enhancing Memory

Ace Frimé
All's Well That Ends Well
Children Don't Have Secrets
Creights
Five And Dime
Gimme
Hold 'Em
Jack-Ass Ate Seven Trees
Kajung
Kings
Spoof
Three-Card Brag

Planning And Problem Solving

Acey-Deucy
Back Alley Bridge
Bezique
Black Maria
Coffee Pot
Crossnumber Puzzle
Dammit
Durak
Four In A Row
Frustration
Gimme
Hold 'Em
In Between
Jackblack
Janet's Challenge
One By One
One Hundred And Fifty
Poker Patience
Three-In-A-Row For Four
Tower Of Hanoi

Fine Motor Skill

Burro Empé

Visual Discrimination, Visual Attention, And Visual Memory

Airplane Solitaire
Asa Pilia Tutto
Back Alley Bridge
Bango
Bichos
Ciao Seppe
Duncan's Trick
Finders Keepers
Hit The Mark
Hockey
Jackass
Jacks Wild
Mariage
Middle Of The Road
Myer's Solitaire
Paul's Game
Piri Picciu
Saskatchewan
Speed
Switch
Turkish Delight

GAMES THAT TEACH BY USING THE CHARACTERISTICS OF A PLAYING CARD

Colour/Number

Add And Subtract
King's Corner
Mariage
Odds Or Evens
Zero

Suit

Four In A Row
Paul's Game
Three-In-A-Row For Four

Number/Suit

Ace Frimé
Acey-Deucey
All Fours
Back Alley Bridge
Big Bango
Black Maria
Burro Empé
Ciao Seppe
Creights
Dammit
Durak
Fallout
Frustration
Gimme
Go To Pack
Hold 'Em
Kajung
King
King's Market
Mark's Place
New Market
Nine-Five-Two
Nine To Zero
One Hundred And Fifty
Piri Picciu
Spoof
Switch
X Marks The Spot
Xeri

Colour/Suit/Number/Letter

Coffee Pot

Number

Asa Pilia Tutto
Add And Subtract
Bichos
Finders Keepers
Guts
Hit The Mark
Hockey
In Between
Jackass
Knuckles
Multiplication Rummy
Ninety-Nine
Odds And Evens
Ronda Robada
Seven And A Half
Speed
Suck The Well
Thirty-One
Three-Card Indian Poker
Turnover Totals

Alphabetic Value

Sentence Rummy

CARD TRICKS

The kids I know love card tricks. They love to be shown them, to learn them, practise them, and perform them. When you show children card tricks you can almost always be sure of having their close attention. They are on the lookout for the fast shuffle, the sly peek, the bottom dealing, or the ace up the sleeve. They want to catch you out, see through the "magic", and figure out how it works.

Not only do card tricks bring about the attentive scrutiny you want kids to cultivate, but discovering the secret behind the "magic" helps develop a sense of logic. Learning to perform brings other intellectual benefits: an emphasis on care and precision — in dealing and fanning and shuffling the cards; memory for a set of procedures or a prescribed patter; a variety of mathematical skills (counting, adding, subtracting, multiplying); and a sense of fun. Furthermore, when a trick is well done, the young magician earns the respect and admiration of friends and relations. This is especially important for children who have not had conventional success in the classroom or on the playground.

None of the following tricks requires special decks of cards from the magic store. Most of the tricks I know, usually taught to me by children, are self-working or mathematical. But the magician has to know the secrets that make them work.

Jailbird's Trick

Ages: 6 - adult

Effect: Magician deals cards in face-down piles, looks at the bottom card of each pile dealt, and occasionally deals cards to a discard pile. After all the cards have been dealt out, spectator is asked to choose any three piles. All other piles are placed on the discard pile. Magician mysteriously removes some of the discards from the stack, counts the rest, and announces the sum of the value of the bottom cards of the three chosen piles.

Magician's secret: While dealing the cards into piles, follow these rules:

Look at the first card; deal it face down. Starting with its number, count on, adding one card until a count of 10 is reached (e.g. if the card is 4, count 5, 6, 7, 8, 9, 10, laying down six cards on the pile). Then begin a new pile in the same manner. Starter cards may be any card from ace through 7. If, as a pile is to be started, any other card is turned up (8, 9, 10, J, Q, K), place it on a discard pile. Continue dealing piles. When dealing the last pile, if the total of 10 cannot be reached, place cards on the discard pile.

At this point, have the spectator choose three piles, placing remainder on discard pile.

Magician then removes nineteen cards from the discard pile and counts the remainder. The number remaining is the total of the bottom cards in the three piles on the table.

Learning skills: careful counting
addition

All's Well That Ends Well

Ages: 6 - adult

Learning this trick can achieve a number of purposes. It can encourage a shy child to perform in public, speak out, and tell a story. The simple story is easy enough for a child with language problems to learn. In the framework of this trick, he will need to follow the structure — to give the beginning, middle, and end, carefully ordering the separate parts in the prescribed sequence. And, for the child who has a problem learning sequences or who has a faulty memory for verbal material, the cards, set up in advance, are literally cue cards for the accompanying story.

This trick might be a good introduction for some children to the idea of using visual prompts to help them remember verbal messages. Pictures, cartoon-like figures, sketches, diagrams, maps, charts, and graphs can all go a long way to help children with problems in verbal memory compensate for their deficits.

Effect: In this trick the magician tells a story, accompanying the narration with a layout of thirty-two cards, which have been prearranged as follows: from the top of the face-down pile to the bottom:

4 aces
4 kings
4 queens
4 hearts (2, 3, 4, 5)
4 diamonds (7, 8, 9, 10)
4 spades (6, 7, 8, 9)
4 jacks
4 clubs (7, 8, 9, 10)

The narration begins:

"Long ago, in the land of Addisabbaba [lay down four aces in a row], there were four kings [lay kings on aces]. Each one loved a queen [lay queens on kings] and wanted to win her heart [lay hearts on queens]. They ordered the royal miners to bring the queens the largest diamonds they could find [lay diamonds on queens]. The miners dug the diamonds up with spades [lay spades on diamonds]. But there were four knaves [bad guys] who saw them [lay jacks on spades]. They chased them with enormous clubs [lay clubs on jacks]. A terrible fight took place and everyone ran away and hid."

As he says the last sentence, the magician picks up the piles, starting from the right, laying one on top of the other. Then he turns the deck over face down and "mixes" the cards, removing a group of cards from the top and placing them on the bottom without disturbing their order. He does this several times. Then he says:

"Later they came back, one at a time, and are all here to tell you their story. Who would you like to see?"

As he is saying this, he deals out a row of eight face-down cards, then deals eight more on the first row, repeating this two more times until there are eight piles of four cards each. Magician glances at the last card before placing it face down.

When the viewers make their request (for kings, queens, diamonds, hearts, etc.), the magician immediately reaches for one of the face-down piles, turns it over, revealing the requested cards.

Magician's secret: Although the exact position of each group will not be known, their relative position is predictable. The piles will be ordered as they appeared in the story: aces, kings, queens, hearts, diamonds, spades, jacks, clubs. By glancing at the last card and knowing what cards are in the last pile, the magician can determine what every other pile contains. For example, if the last card is a heart, the magician knows the preceding piles are, from right to left, Q, K, A, clubs, jacks, spades, and diamonds.

Learning skills: ordering a story
                     language facility
                     discovering aids for faulty verbal memory

Queens On Top

Ages: 7 - adult

Effect: Magician introduces this as a story for the 80's, when women have managed to prove their excellence in every field they enter. He hands a spectator a full deck of cards and gives the following instructions: "Divide the deck into four approximately equal piles." (He demonstrates that this is done by dropping piles off the bottom from left to right so that the top quarter of the deck is the right-most pile.) Pick up the first pile (at the left) and deal down the top three cards in its place, then deal the next three cards to the top of each of the next three other piles. Replace the remaining cards of the pile onto the three cards holding its place. Repeat this with each of the three other piles (three cards down, then one to each of the other piles, then replace the pile). After the fourth pile has been dealt out this way, turn up the top card of each pile. There, demonstrating the power of women to rise to the top, are the four queens.

Magician's secret: Before handing the deck to the spectator, magician has secretly placed the four queens on top. After that the trick works itself.

Learning skills: following instructions
language facility
number concepts

Add It Up First

Ages: 8 - adult

Effect: Magician has someone pick a card. Then, going through the deck once, looking at each card, the magician can name the card that was removed.

Magician's secret: Keep a running total of the cards, but every time the total goes above 13, subtract 13.

Value of cards: All cards from A to 9 have their face value. Kings = 0; for a 10 subtract 3; for a J subtract 2; for a Q subtract 1.

Subtract the final total from 13 to get the value of the missing card. If the result is 11, the missing card is a jack; if 12, a queen; and if 0, a king.

A magician prepared to practise can make this trick more dazzling by naming the suit as well. But in that case the trick has to be done, sitting down — the secret is in the feet.

Magician starts with both feet flat on the floor. As he turns the cards and calculates the face value, he notes the suit. For each spade that turns up he raises or lowers his left heel. For a club he raises or lowers his right heel. For each heart he changes both feet at once. (Be careful here, especially if both are in different positions.) No change at all is made for diamonds.

At the end of the deal the position of the feet indicates the missing card.

Left heel up (right down):   a spade
Right heel up (left down):   a club
Both heels up: a heart
Both heels down: a diamond

Learning skills: addition
                     subtraction
                     right and left discrimination

X-Ray Vision

Ages: 8 - adult

Effect: Without watching, the magician instructs a member of the audience: "Cut the deck in half. Discard half. Count the remaining cards. Add the digits of that total together. Discard that many cards. Pick any number from 1 to 9. Count down that many cards from the deck and place them in your pocket. Now count down the same number and see what card is in that position, without removing it." Magician turns around. Given the remaining pack, the magician counts the cards in it, and then tells the audience how many cards are in the pocket and names the chosen card.

Magician's secret: When the magician receives the remaining cards, he counts them and adds the two digits of their total together. Then he subtracts that number from 9 and gets the total in the pocket. That also gives the position of the chosen card so that it can be pulled out from the pack — to the complete amazement of the audience.

Learning skills: addition
subtraction

There are many unsubstantiated theories about the origins of playing cards in China or India, but no real proof. There is, however, documented evidence that playing cards were used in Europe in 1377. A treatise in Latin, written by a German monk, describes the game of cards. Along with describing the game he suggests that in it "there is a moral action of the virtues and vices"; "it is of service for mental relief and rest to the tired"; "it is useful for idle persons and may be a comfort to them".

As The Ox Ploughs

Ages: 6 -adult

Boustrophedon was an early form of writing that went back and forth across the page, left to right (as the ox ploughs). The deal of the card in this trick is reminiscent of that writing style.

Effect: Magician deals out twenty-one cards face up in three piles. Spectator is asked to choose one of the cards during the deal and note its location. After being told in what pile the chosen card is located, magician picks up the cards. He redeals them twice more, each time being told the location of the chosen card. Magician then deals the cards face down and, without looking, selects one. Before turning it over he asks the spectator to name the card that had been chosen. Then he turns the selected card over to reveal the card that has been named.

Magician's secret: Magician deals cards into three piles from left to right (1-2-3) and then right to left (3-2-1) back and forth until all twenty-one cards are dealt out. Spectator tells magician in which pile the chosen card is located. Magician picks up piles, putting the pile with the chosen card between the other two. Cards are redealt twice, using the back and forth dealing. Each time spectator tells magician which pile contains the chosen card. That pile is put between the other two. After that, magician deals the cards face down counting silently to himself. He pauses just before the eleventh card, asks the spectator to name the card he has chosen, then turns over the eleventh card. This is the card that had been selected.

Learning skills: right and left discrimination
careful counting
concepts of forward and backward

Children Don't Have Secrets

Ages: 8 - adult

It may seem impossible for a child who has problems learning lists by heart to memorize the order of fifty-two cards in a deck. Well, with a little deviousness on his part, some elementary arithmetic, and the ability to remember the sentence at the top of the page, he can convince his friends that he has an amazing memory.

Effect: Magician presents a member of the audience with a deck of cards and asks that the cards be cut any number of times (remember, a *cut*, not a shuffle).

Then audience member is asked to look at the top card in the deck, name it, and magician correctly names the card that is next to it.

Audience member replaces cards, cuts again, announces the new top card, and once again magician correctly tells the card that is below it. This may be repeated a number of times until it is clear that the magician really knows the order of the cards.

Magician's secret: Magician has "stacked" the deck, that is, arranged the cards in an order that is not easily spotted as an ordered arrangement, but an order that can be easily remembered.

The cards are arranged as follows:
    3 of clubs
    6 of diamonds
    9 of hearts
    Q of spades
    2 of clubs
    5 of diamonds
    8 of hearts
    J of spades
    A of clubs
    4 of diamonds
    7 of hearts
    10 of spades
    K of clubs
    3 of diamonds

6 of hearts
9 of spades
Q of clubs
2 of diamonds
5 of hearts
8 of spades
J of clubs
A of diamonds
4 of hearts
7 of spades
10 of clubs
K of diamonds
3 of hearts
6 of spades
9 of clubs
Q of diamonds
2 of hearts
5 of spades
etc.

The denomination of the cards is increased by three (a 3 is followed by a six, a 10 is followed by a king, a jack is followed by an ace, a queen is followed by a 2, a king is followed by a 3) and the suits follow each other in the order of clubs, diamonds, hearts, spades (*Children Don't Have Secrets* is a phrase where the first letter of each word helps you remember the order).

Thus, when any card is named, the magician can predict the following card. If the card named is 4 of diamonds, magician thinks "4 + 3 = 7; diamonds = Don't, followed by Have = hearts." So the next card is 7 of hearts. If the card named is Q of clubs, magician thinks "king, ace, *two*, clubs = Children, followed by Don't = diamonds." So the next card is 2 of diamonds.

Learning skills: memory development
addition (increments of 3)
ordering

Five And Dime

Ages: 8 - adult

Effect: Magician asks for two volunteers. Each one is dealt a pile of twelve face-down cards. On the table the magician places a nickel and a dime. Then he turns his back. Players are asked to choose one of two coins, and one card each from their face-down packs. Each is asked to multiply the number of his card by the value of his coin and announce the total of the two answers. Magician immediately names each player's coin.

Magician's secret: Magician has prearranged the deck so that the first twelve cards are odd and the next twelve cards are even. This ensures that all the cards dealt to player A are odd, and to player B even.

If the figure given to the magician is even, the person who got the odd card has the dime. If the number is odd, the person who got the odd card has the nickel.

Mathematics:

A	B	
10×3	5×4	$= 50$

Even number, therefore player A has the dime.

Learning skills: mental computation
ordering
learning money denominations
understanding "odd" and "even"

Janet's Challenge

Ages: 5 - adult

Effect: Challenger holds up the thirteen cards of a suit, so that the viewer can see that the cards are not in any logical order. Then, with the packet face down and dealing from the top, challenger places a card on the bottom of the deck, and faces up the next card and lays it on the table (an ace); then he puts the next one on the bottom and faces up the next, a two. This continues, with cards alternated, one under, one on the table, until all thirteen cards have been dealt out in order from ace to king.

Spectator is challenged to do the same. Figuring out the initial "random" arrangement is an excellent exercise for young teenagers. The "trick" itself can be done even by very young children once the arrangement has been made.

Magician's Secret: The prearrangement is below, but I hope you will try to figure it out yourself.

Prearrangement: 7 A Q 2 8 3 J 4 9 5 K 6 10

Learning skills: problem solving
practice in alternation
ordering

There were three different kinds of suit-markings in Europe. Italian cards had swords, clubs (real clubs, the kind you wield), cups, and coins. German cards had acorns, leaves, hearts, and bells. Our cards developed from the French cards which had the markings we know as clubs, spades, hearts, and diamonds.

Duncan's Trick

Ages: 8 - adult

Effect: Magician lays out five rows of five cards each. Someone chooses a card and tells magician which row it is in. Magician picks up cards seemingly at random, then lays them down again in a five-by-five array. Again, a row is named. Magician picks up the chosen card.

Magician's secret: Magician picks up cards at random, except that the fifth, ninth, thirteenth, seventeenth, and twenty-first come from the designated row. When they are laid down again in rows of five each, cards from the chosen row form a diagonal from the right. As soon as the spectator chooses his row, the magician can select the key card from that row.

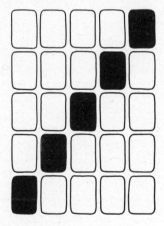

Learning skills: careful counting
spatial relations

Spatial Relations/Colour

Ages: 8 - adult

Effect: Magician lays out sixteen face-up cards in four rows of four and writes down the name of one of the cards and gives it to a member of the audience to hold.

The magician gives the following set of instructions, each incorporating a choice, to a volunteer:

1. Put a small object on any red card.
2. Move it left or right to the nearest black card.
3. Move it vertically up or down to the nearest red card.
4. Move it diagnoally to the nearest black card.
5. Move it down (toward self) or to the right to the nearest red card.

Magician calls for the name of the card given to the audience and it is revealed as the card on which the object is.

Magician's secret: The magician's secret is her sure-fire arrangement of cards;

black	red	red	red
red	black	black	black
red	black	(red)	red
red	black	black	black

No matter where the object is placed initially it will end up in the circled slot. It is the name of the card in this position that the magician writes down.

Learning skills: directional awareness
spatial concepts
remembering an ordered set of instructions

Spatial Relations/Odd And Even

Ages: 8 - adult

Effect: This trick calls for consideration of odd and even numbers rather than colour. Again, sixteen cards are laid out, face-up in four rows of four. The magician predicts the name of a card and then gives the following instructions to a member of the audience:
1. Put a small object on any even card.
2. Move left or right to nearest odd card.
3. Move vertically up or down to nearest even card.
4. Move diagonally to nearest odd card.
5. Move down or to the right to the nearest even card.
Magician's prediction is confirmed.

Magician's secret: Again the arrangement of the cards allows for the prediction to be true no matter which choices of movement are made.

odd	even	even	even
even	odd	odd	odd
even	odd	(even)	even
even	odd	odd	odd

Learning skills: spatial awareness
right and left discrimination
concept of "odd" and "even"
remembering an ordered set of instructions

Dealer's Choice

Ages: 7 - adult

Effect: Count out sixteen cards from the deck, but do not indicate that the number of cards has any significance. Spread them out face down on the table and ask someone to pick a card. Look at it. Place it on top of the rest of the deck, and place the remaining fifteen cards from the spread on the top card. Now ask the volunteer to remove the top half of the deck (an approximate cut in half will do). Discard the bottom half. Take remaining cards, the top half, and deal the cards out between you into two face-down piles — the first to her, the next to you, until the cards are dealt out. Then take your own pile and deal the cards out from top to bottom face down in front of you (so that the order is reversed). Pick them up and deal them between you as before. Again deal your cards from top to bottom in front of you, reversing the order. Continue dealing and reversing until you are left with one card.

Ask for the name of the selected card. Turn over your card to reveal that you have mysteriously found it.

Challenge to the magician: *Do you know how you did it?*

Learning skills: careful counting
                       ordering

The United States Playing Card Company makes a line of cards that can be used by people with up to 95% visual impairment. The numbers on them are twice the size of the numbers on conventional playing cards, and two additional colours — blue and green — are used to help players who are unable to distinguish the suit markings. The cards are called E-Z See/Lo-Vision Cards.

Over-Under

Age: 6 - adult

Effect: Take ace through 10 of one suit, arranging them in numerical order from ace to 10, with ace on the top and 10 on the bottom.

Say that you will deal the cards onto the table into a pile according to the spectator's instructions of "over" or "under". If the command is "over", deal the card directly onto the pile; if "under", slip the card under the next top card and then take both of them off the deck and place them on the pile.

Continue to deal as instructed, picking up the cards on the table and repeating two or three times. Then ask if the viewers agree that the cards are now completely out of order. Now tap the deck, saying that you will restore them to their original order. Turn up the cards and, just as you promised, they are ordered from ace to 10.

Magician's secret: This trick always works.

Challenge to the magician: *Figure out why.*

Learning skills: ordering
spatial relations

When the Astronauts orbited the earth they had special fireproof cards — versions of the Bicycle cards made by the U.S. Playing Card Company.

A good deck of cards to take on a camping trip is a deck called *Survival* Cards. Each playing card features an important and useful tip for coping with an outdoor emergency. Survival playing cards are produced by Environs, Inc. Route 2, Box 508, Hood River, Oregon.

Magic Fingers

Ages: 8 - adult

Effect: Produce a deck of cards. Ask a spectator to deal cards from the top of the deck onto a pile until about halfway through the deck. Have spectator shuffle the two halves together using a riffle shuffle. A riffle shuffle is done by releasing cards by your thumbs so that the cards interweave. Announce that you have sensitive fingertips that can feel colours. To demonstrate this you will, without looking, produce from this shuffled deck pairs of cards, with each pair always composed of a card of each colour — one red and one black. You put the deck behind your back and pull out cards two at a time. Just as you promised, they always consist of one black card and one red card.

Magician's secret: Before presenting this trick you have prearranged the deck, alternating the cards in colour — one red, one black, one red, one black, and so on. When you put the cards behind your back you simply take the first two cards off the top. One will be red and one will be black. Then take the next two off the top, and so on. Each pair will contain a red and a black card.

Some thoughts for the magician: *While rehearsing this trick without an audience, you might look at the cards after you have shuffled them. Does shuffling upset the alternating arrangement you have set up? Why does the trick work?*
This is a trick that does not allow you to let the spectator see the deck in advance. The alternating colour arrangement is very obvious and the spectator would see immediately that the deck had been prearranged. I had a bright idea for a variation on this trick that would allow for a set-up that was not so obvious. This was to alternate odd and even cards (regardless of colour), then demonstrate that your sensitive fingers could read the cards and always produce a pair that contained an odd card and an even card. When I tried to arrange the deck I realized that it wouldn't work. Can you figure out why? What would we have to do to make it work? (Hint: How many odd cards in the deck? How many even cards? Jacks = 11, queens = 12, kings = 13)

Learning skills: alternation
ordering
logical thinking

Middle Of The Road

Ages: 8 - adult

Effect: Give a spectator a number of cards. Turn your back and tell him to deal them onto the table face up in three equal columns. Tell him to choose a card in one of the columns, pick up that column, shuffle it well. Then, making a pile of each of the columns, he is to place the chosen pile between the other two. Then he is to take this pack and deal the cards face up as though he were dealing cards one at a time to five players. When there are five face-up hands on the table, turn around and ask him to indicate which "hand" contains his card. You point to the card.

Magician's secret: You have given the spectator exactly fifteen cards. With this number, the chosen card will always be the middle one of the three-card hand.

Learning skills: careful counting
spatial relations

Pick A Card

First of all: Take twenty-seven cards from a deck of fifty-two. Ask a spectator to pick a card as you deal out the cards without letting you know what it is.

Effect: Deal three face-up cards to start three separate piles. Then, on each pile, deal cards in turn until there are three piles of nine cards each. Ask which pile contains the chosen card. Take up the cards one pile at a time, placing the pile with the chosen card between the other two.

Deal the cards again as before. Again ask for the location of the chosen card. Pick up the piles with the key pile in the middle. Deal one more time using the same method. When the pile containing the chosen card is indicated, reach for the card and amaze your audience.

Magician's secret: As cards are dealt out the final time, note the fifth (middle) card in each pile. When the pile is named, simply remove the fifth card in that pile.

Hint to the magician: *Try to pick up the card without obviously counting. Just go directly to it. What I do to remember those three cards is to say their names in order to myself as I deal out the remaining cards, e.g., "6 of clubs, 7 of hearts, 3 of diamonds; 6 of clubs, 7 of hearts, 3 of diamonds". Then, when the spectator says "second pile", I immediately reach for the seven of hearts without having to count the cards in the pile.*

Learning skills: following directions
careful counting
spatial relations
verbal rehearsal

Jack-Ass Ate Seven Trees

Age: 6 - adult

First of all: Order the cards in a deck as follows: jack, ace, 8, 7, 3, king, 10, 2, 6, 5, 4, 9, queen (and start over again from the jack) with the suits ordered as clubs, hearts, spades, diamonds. Thus, the jack of clubs will be followed by the ace of hearts, followed by the 8 of spades, and so on.

Effect: When shown any card in the deck, magician can tell the following card.

Magician's secret: How does the magician remember the order of cards when there is no numerical pattern to the sequence? Simple — by learning this pair of sentences:

> Jack(J)-Ass (A) ate (8) seven (7) trees (3). King (K) inTENds (10) to (2) fix (6) five (5) for (4) benign (9) Queen (Q).

and by remembering this word: CHaSeD. The consonants are in the same order as the suits (*c*lubs, *h*earts, *s*pades, *d*iamonds).

Thus, if the magician turned up the seven of hearts, he would think ". . . seven trees . . ." and know the next card was a 3; then he would think "CHaSeD" and know that after a heart comes a spade. Therefore, the card next in line must be the 3 of spades.

Special consideration: *If the word "benign" seems too far removed from the experience of the child learning the trick, or if it is too hard to remember — thereby defeating the purpose of the mnemonic — then substitute the word "fine".*

Learning skills: memory skills
ordering
language facility
practice making verbal associations

Fifty-two Minus X

Ages: 10 - adult

Effect: Fan a deck of fifty-two cards (make sure jokers are removed) so that cards are face up. Ask a spectator to pick a card at random and place it on the bottom of the deck. Leave the deck face down so you cannot possibly see the card. Ask the spectator to choose a number between twenty and forty. Let's say thirty is chosen. Now ask the spectator to deal that number of cards (thirty), first demonstrating how you want the cards dealt. After the demonstration the spectator deals thirty cards, turns up the thirtieth, and it is the selected card.

Magician's secret: When the spectator picks a number, mentally subtract that number from fifty-two. In the example above you would get $52 - 30 = 22$. In demonstrating to the spectator how you want the cards dealt, deal 22 cards off the top. To cover the fact that you are counting cards, say that you want cards dealt one at a time (illustrate, counting to yourself all the while), not in groups of two or three or four (demonstrate, but keep counting). When you have your twenty-two, place the deck on top of that pile and ask the spectator to deal cards equal to the number he selected.

Hint to the magician: *Before you do this trick, practise silent counting and talking at the same time.*

Learning skills: mental computation
subtraction

Some of the baffling card tricks done by magicians are done with a "stripper" deck. This is a deck that is very slightly tapered so that one end of the deck is narrower than the other. The difference is hardly visible to the eye, but when a card is reversed in the deck, the magician's fingers can immediately detect it.

Jokers Out

Ages: 10 - adult

Effect: After removing the jokers from a shuffled deck of cards, ask the spectator to remove a few cards (under twenty) from the top of the deck and put them aside where you can't see them. Then ask him to look at the top card of the deck, remember it, and cut the cards so that that card is now somewhere in the middle. You turn over the deck, fan the cards, cut the deck. Now you ask the spectator to tell you how many cards he took off the top. Then you ask him to deal that many cards off the deck and to turn over the last card. That will be the card he picked.

Magician's secret: While you are removing the jokers, note the bottom card of the deck and remember it. Let's say it is the jack of diamonds. Beginning with that card, count twenty cards (don't be obvious). Cut the cards at the twentieth card so that the jack of diamonds is now twenty cards from the top.

After the spectator has removed the cards, noted the top card, and cut the cards, you look at the face-up deck. While doing so, you find the jack of diamonds, count back nineteen cards (again, do this without it being obvious that you are counting), cut the cards at that point, and place that packet on top of the deck. When the spectator counts down the number of cards he has removed, the chosen card will be there.

Hint to the magician: *Practise this trick, counting silently and handling cards casually so that no one can tell you are counting.*

Challenge to the magician: *Figure out why this works.*

Learning skills: mental computation

SOLITAIRES

Having a stock of games of Solitaire is a useful source of diversion for children who need to do something with their hands, eyes, and minds. A game of solitaire can be a boon to children who might otherwise have to resort to obstreperous or intrusive behaviour to keep their motors fueled.

I have never met a game of Solitaire I didn't like. There is something very satisfying in starting with disorder — a random arrangement of cards — and watching order restored, as the cards fall into a special pattern, or change places according to a plan, or form an ordered sequence from ace through king.

Frequently, the layout of a game of Solitaire teaches number facts. For instance, an array of cards may illustrate 1 x 1 = 16.

Myer's Solitaire

Ages: 10 - adult

In this game, cards are arranged in overlapping rows, so that the numbers and suits of all upturned cards are visible. It is a good game to help a child learn the orderly habits necessary to set his arithmetic examples down neatly and to align columns carefully. If the cards are laid down sloppily, play becomes impossible. Player must continually "neaten" his cards, restoring separate columns and rearranging the cards so that their suit and denomination are always visible.

Object of the game: Playing same suit cards onto eligible cards in descending order until all four suits are arranged in four piles from king to ace.

Layout: All of the cards are dealt in overlapping rows of seven each, with the last three cards forming their own row. Cards are dealt as follows:

First four rows: three face-up cards; four face-down cards
Next three rows: seven face-up cards
Last row: three face-up cards.

The result is seven columns: the first three with eight overlapping face-up cards, the last four with four face-down, and three face-up overlapping cards.

Play: Cards at the bottom of each column may be played upon. Play consists of placing cards of the same suit in descending order. Any visible card is eligible for play, but must be moved from its column and put in place with all the cards below it. Moving cards makes new cards eligible to be played on.

If a column becomes empty, any visible king may be placed in that spot. When the face-down cards are reached by moving the cards below them, they are turned over and brought into play.

When no more moves are possible, cards are picked up, one column at a time, from left to right (turning over the face-down cards so that all cards face the same way) and redealt in the original arrangement. Play is resumed.

This can go on indefinitely.

Game is won when all four suits are arranged in four piles from king to ace.

Tips: *To minimize frustration in this infrequently won solitaire, it can be taught with the assignment to discover how many deals it takes to win. Children playing Solitaire alongside friends can compare notes.*

It often seems, at first glance, that a new layout offers no moves. Then careful scrutiny reveals a single play.

Suddenly moving one lot of cards to a new location leads to four or five moves in quick succession. Sometimes players must decide which of two moves should be made first. One move may lead to more possibilities for play. Similarly, if there is a slot for a king and more than one king to choose from, player will want to anticipate the moves resulting from each choice, and then choose the one that seems to offer the most possibilities for play.

Variations:
1) When no plays are possible, an eighth column may be started by moving one of the last four columns of face-up cards and turning up the top face-down card. This may give new playing possibilities.
2) When there is an empty column and no king available for the slot, one of the last four columns of face-up cards may be moved into the slot, allowing one of the face-down cards to be available for play.
3) When there is an empty column, player may choose between an available king and one of the four face-down columns of cards to fill the slot. If player sees that moving the king is not likely to open up many possibilities for play, he may prefer to take a chance on a new card.
4) For more frequent wins, play the game using all of the above variations.

Learning skills: ordering
visual scanning
necessity for neatness
persistence

Jane's Grandmother's Solitaire

Ages: 6 - adult

Layout: Deal four face-up cards in a square.

Value of cards: Aces are high.

Object of the game: To remove cards and to be left with only the four aces.

Play: If two or more face-up cards are of the same suit, remove the lower card(s). Deal four more cards, covering the cards in the layout or the spaces that remain. After each deal, whenever there are cards of the same suit, always remove the cards lower in value. If a space becomes available, the top card of any pile may be used to fill the space. Before dealing the next four cards, always check for possible removals. Deal out all the cards. The game is won when only the four aces are left.

Learning skills: classification
relative value of numbers

One writer on cards says that ace means money, and that the card is traditionally more valuable than the king in card games because the king would be powerless without money. Another account says that, during the Renaissance, society came to realize that the king exists to serve the people — therefore the lowest common man is more powerful than the king, and in cards the ace takes precedence over the king.

Plus Or Minus One

Ages: 5 - adult

Object of the game: To build all the cards into a single pile by playing on cards (regardless of suit) that are one higher or one lower than the face-up card. (A king may be played on an ace and an ace on a king.)

Play: Hold the deck face-down and deal the top card face up to the table to start the "build". Turn up cards one at a time. If the turned-up card is one less or one greater than the face-up "build" card, it is played face-up on the pile. If not, it is played to a discard pile. Play continues until all cards are dealt out. Then the discard pile is turned over and play resumed.

The "official" rules call for two additional redeals of the deck. Since the game is seldom won in this version I have modified it. I allow unlimited redeals until no more plays can be made. When a game is won, count the number of runthroughs of the deck it took. When the game is lost, count how many cards are left in the discard pile. By keeping track of how many times the deck has been dealt for wins and how many left-overs for losses, the child has an interesting record, as well as many opportunities to learn by heart the result of adding or subtracting one to the numbers from 2 to 13.

Plus Or Minus Two

This is played exactly like "Plus Or Minus One", except that the increment between cards is 2. Thus, on a 6 you may play an 8 or a 4; on a 3, an A or a 5. On a queen, you may play a 10 (-2) or an ace ($+2$); on a king you may play a jack (-2) or a 2 ($+2$).

For children who are adept at arithmetic, or for those who want to develop computational skill, the possibilities are obvious: "Plus or Minus 3", "Plus or Minus 4", "Plus or Minus 5".

Learning skills: addition
subtraction

Sevens

Ages: 9 - adult

Equipment: A deck of cards.

Object of the game: To get rid of all the cards.

Value of cards: Ace to 10 equal their face value; jack = 11; queen = 12; king = 13.

Play: Deal cards in a row. Remove, as they are faced up, sevens and all adjacent cards that total any multiple of seven.

Learning skills: addition
multiplication (7 times table)

Nines

Ages: 6 - adult

This is a good addition to anybody's repertoire of solitaires that provide practice in computation. What I do for the player who doesn't know number facts off by heart is provide a key — a sheet of paper with the needed sums written out $(8+1=9; 7+2=9; 6+3=9; 5+4=9)$. After a few deals of "Nines", even the chronic forgetters of number facts have memorized the combinations of numbers that equal nine.

Equipment: A deck of cards.

Layout: Deal nine face-up cards in three rows of three.

Play: Cover, with face-up cards from the pack, any two cards that total 9. Cover any single 9's. Cover 10, jack, queen, king whenever two of these of the same suit are exposed. Continue covering the designated cards until there are no cards that can be covered (in which case the game is lost), or until the entire deck is dealt out. Then pick up the piles that would normally be covered — pairs where the top cards total 9, a pile with 9 as the top card, two piles with any same suit 10, J, Q, or K. If there are no remaining piles the game is won.

Learning skills: addition

Witch's Brew

Ages: 7 - adult

Object of the game: To get rid of as many cards as possible and to have remaining cards of the lowest possible value; to play as many hands as possible before reaching a total of 100.

Equipment: A deck of cards.

Value of cards: Kings, Queens, and Jacks are equal to 10. All other cards are equal to their face value.

Layout: Cards are dealt face up in a horizontal row in front of the player. Play begins as soon as two cards are available for play.

Play: Cards at either end of the line are available for play. Remove two or more adjacent cards or cards at the beginning or end of the row that total 11, 12, or 13. Thus, if the layout began 6, 9, J, Q, 7, you could remove the 7 and the 6 (= 13). If the next card were an ace, you could remove the ace and queen (= 11). When all cards have been dealt out and all possible plays have been made, add up the total of the cards remaining in the layout. When your total reaches 100, you have lost.

Learning skills: addition

Places

Ages: 5 - adult

A game for one, but fun for two, three, or four players to play out simultaneously to see who can be the first to be successful.

Object of the game: To turn up all the cards.

First of all: Take the cards ace through 7 of one suit. Mix the cards thoroughly and deal them out face down in front of you.

Play: Player may first turn up either the second or third card from either end. The denomination of the turned-up card determines the position of the next card he may face up. For example, if it is a 4 he may turn up the *fourth* card from either end. If it is an ace he may turn up the *first* card at either end. When the next card is faced up it determines the position of the next card to be turned over, and so on.

Play continues until all cards are faced up or until play is stopped because cards in the designated positions have already been turned over.

Variations: This game can be made a little simpler by decreasing the number of cards (to the first five, for example), or it can be made a little more challenging by increasing the numbers to include the entire suit with jack standing for 11, queen for 12, and king for 13.

Learning skills: visual-spatial concepts
numerical ordering

Airplane Solitaire I

Ages: 6 - adult

Play: Cards are turned up one at a time, and player "counts" in synchrony — A through K — repeating the count four times, if possible. Game is lost if the card "name" recited aloud ever agrees with the card that is turned up as the name is said.

Airplane Solitaire II

Play: Cards are turned up one at a time and player "counts" in synchrony, reciting the card names in sequence — ace through king. This is repeated throughout the game. If a card and name agree (that is, if a 6, for example, turns up as the player is saying "six"), the card is removed from the deck.

The object of the game is to remove all the cards. When player has gone through the deck he turns the cards over, continuing the count from the point at which he left off. Play continues until the game is won or no more plays are possible. This occurs when the deck always begins at the same count because no cards have been removed on the previous runthrough of the cards.

Learning skills: counting
sequencing
visual discrimination

Airplane Factors I

Ages: 9 - adult

Value of cards: A – 10 = face value; J = 11, Q = 12, K = 13.

Play: Player turns up cards one at a time, counting by twos. If, at any time, the number spoken is divisible by the number on the card turned up simultaneously, the card is discarded. For example if, as a player says "fifty-six" and turns up a 7 (56 ÷ 7 = 8), the card is removed from the pack. When the pack has been gone through once, player goes through it again, this time counting by 3's, then by 4's, then by 5's.

Learning skills: counting in groups
multiplication facts
division

Airplane Factors II

Value of cards: A – 10 = face value; J = 11; Q = 12; K = 13.

Play: Player turns up cards one at a time. As he turns each card he recites the multiplication tables (if he does not know them off by heart, he may want to have a chart or matrix handy), starting with 1 × 1 through 1 × 12, then continuing with the two-times table, then the three-times table, and so on, up to 12 × 12. When the pack has been gone through, the cards are picked up and redealt, continuing the recitation from where it left off. Whenever the product recited aloud is a multiple of the card simultaneously faced up, then the card is removed from the pack. (For example, if player says 6 × 4 = 24 and a queen is turned up, it is removed because 12 × 2 = 24.) The object of the game is to remove all the cards.

Learning skills: multiplication

Turkish Delight

Ages: 5 - adult

In Turkey this is a fortune telling game. You make a wish before you start. If you win the game it is a sign your wish might come true.

Layout: Deal out the entire deck in thirteen piles of four face-down cards, turn up the top card on each pile.

Object of the game: To get rid of all the cards by removing them in pairs.

Play: Remove cards in pairs (cards of the same denomination), turning up the card that is uncovered with each removal. Continue until all cards are removed or no move is possible.

Learning skills: number recognition
                      matching

Calendar Solitaire

Ages: 7 - 12

Object of the game: To get rid of all the cards.

First of all: Remove the four kings from the deck.

Value of cards: Jacks = 11, queens = 12.

Play: Cards are turned over one at a time and player, in synchrony with card turning, recites the months of the year. As first card is turned up he says "January"; as second card is turned up he says "February"; and so on. This is repeated, starting the recitation over when the twelve months have been named until all the cards have been turned up.

Whenever the number of a card turned up is the same as the number of the month that is named (i.e., January = 1, February = 2, March = 3, etc.) it is removed from the deck.

When all the cards have been turned over, the deck is picked up and redealt, with "count" resumed from the point at which it was stopped. For example, if, as the last card was turned over, player said "February," then, as the deal resumes, player says "March."

Variation: Make object of the game to get through the deck without having number turned up and number of month ever coincide (this makes for much shorter play!).

Modifications:
1. For a player who has not yet learned the months in sequence, provide a numbered list of the months to refer to while playing.
2. For non-readers, provide a tape of months of the year recited in sequence, slowly and rhythmically; "January, one; February, two; March, three,", etc. Let the child synchronize laying down of the cards with the voice on tape, and play as directed.

Learning skills: learning the months and their position in the calendar year

Four-Leaf Clover

Ages: 7 - adult

First of all: Remove the 10's from the deck, leaving forty-eight cards.

Layout: Deal sixteen cards, face up, in four rows of four.

Value of cards: J = 11, Q = 12, K = 13, other cards = face value.

Play: Remove from this array two or more cards of the same suit totalling 15. Replace with cards from the stack. Game is won if all forty-eight cards are removed in play.

Variation: Remove aces from the deck. Deal sixteen cards face up in four rows of four. Remove pairs of same-colour cards that total 15.

Learning skills: addition

70

Family Reunion

Ages: 10 - adult

Object of the game: To lay out the cards for the foundation (described below) and then build the rest in downward suit sequence from jacks to twos.

Equipment: One deck of cards.

Layout: Deal out a rectangular "fence" of sixteen cards, with four at the top, four arranged vertically down each side and four at the bottom. Make sure there is room for a circular foundation of eight cards inside the "fence".

Play: Cards are moved, where possible, from the layout. The foundation cards themselves are moved in pairs and to particular positions as follows: king and queen of each suit, with queen placed on top of king: club pairs are at the North (top); spades at the South (bottom); hearts at the West (left); diamonds at the East (right). Jacks and aces (moved together, with jack on top) are placed next to their queen's position preceding them in clockwise rotation (i.e., clubs northwest, diamonds northeast, spades southeast, and hearts southwest).

If cards have been moved from the layout, the spaces are refilled from the pack. The pack is dealt one card at a time to a face-up discard pile. Plays are made where possible to the foundation. Cards may be dealt only once in the official rules. I prefer at least one redeal so that the game may be won a little more often.

Learning skills: ordering
                                    visual-spatial concepts
                                    names of cardinal directions

Queen Bee

Ages: 8 - adult

I have a confession to make. I first heard of this two-deck solitaire under the title Shah. *The object of the game was to complete a layout that resulted in the King of Hearts (the Shah) surrounded by the eight Queens — his harem. I found the sexist implications most unsuitable in a game for children. So I have revised it slightly and renamed it.*

Equipment: 2 decks of cards. Remove all Kings and all Queens except the Queen of Clubs.

Layout: Place the Queen of Clubs in the centre of the table and arrange the eight Aces around it to make a spoke-like pattern.

Object of the game: To build sequences in suit, on the Aces to the Jacks, so that if the game is won, the Queen Bee will be surrounded by eight drones — the Jacks.

Play: Place a card next to each Ace. If any of the cards is a 2, place it on a same-suit Ace and fill in the vacancy. Repeat this until there are 3 cards next to each Ace making eight four-card spokes; always replacing any card that is placed on the foundation.

Any end card is available for play. Cards may then be taken from the end of each spoke and placed in descending sequence on same-suit cards on the end.

When all possible plays have been made, the stock is turned up, one card at a time. Cards may be placed on the ace piles in ascending suit sequence or on the end cards in descending suit sequence. Otherwise, they are played to a discard pile.

If all the cards of a spoke next to the ace become vacant, the space can be filled by an end card from another spoke.

Variation: A simpler, but quite satisfying, version may be played by younger children using a single deck with kings and three queens.

Learning skills: ordering
                     visual-spatial concepts

Copy-Cat

Ages: 8 - adult

Deal one face-up card — the "leader". To the left of that card, deal a pile of five cards — four face-down cards, and the top one face up. Below that, in a vertical column, make three more five-card piles (four face down, top one face up).

Cards from the stock are turned up one at a time and played in rows adjacent to the piles as follows: the leader card determines the suit of the first row. Any card of that suit may be played beside it in an overlapping row. The leader card determines the denomination of the first card of each of the three subsequent rows. As soon as a card of the same denomination is turned up it is played in the second row. The next card of the leader card's denomination begins the third row, and the remaining one of that rank begins the fourth. A card may be played only if there is already a card of the same denomination in the row above. When one of the face-up cards on the left is eligible for play, it is played and the card below is faced up.

When all the cards from the stock have been dealt out, turn them over and continue to play until no more plays are available.

Game is won if all cards have been played.

Learning skills: visual discrimination
ordering

Quadrille

Ages: 6 - adult

My favourite solitaire as a child was "Three's in the Corner" and I have taught it to hundreds of children who needed practice in moving up and down the number line. I only recently discovered "Quadrille". It calls on similar skills, but is much prettier and somehow reminds me of Alice in Wonderland.

Layout: Arrange four queens in the centre as a cross, with the queen of spades at the north, queen of clubs at the south, queen of hearts to the east, and queen of diamonds to the west. This is only to create a pleasing tableau, but the learning of the formula and the arranging of it will help the player's sense of direction and map-reading ability.

Around the queens arrange the 5's and 6's, with the 5 of spades to the north of the queen of spades, the 6 of spades to the northeast; the 5 of hearts to the east of the queen of hearts, the 6 of hearts to the south-east; the 5 of clubs to the south of the queen of clubs, the 6 of clubs to the southwest; the five of diamonds to the west of the queen of diamonds and the 6 of diamonds to the northwest.

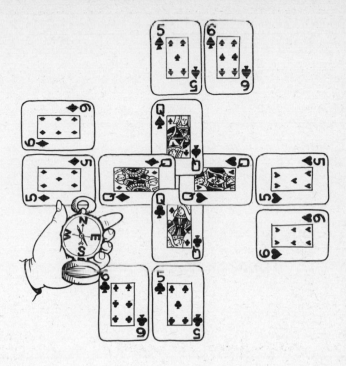

Object of the game: To build upwards in suit on the 6's to the jacks; to build downwards in suit on the 5's to kings (5-4-3-2-A-K).

Play: Turn up cards from the deck one at a time and place them on the appropriate builds where possible, or turn them face up on a trash (discard) pile.

When all the cards have been dealt out they may be redealt. Three redeals are permissible.

Learning skills: numerical ordering
learning the cardinal directions, north, south,
east, and west

Saskatchewan

Ages: 5 - 10

Layout: Deal a row of eight face-up cards (or, for variety, two rows of four face-up cards).

Object of the game: To deal out all the cards.

Play: With the cards remaining in the deck, cover cards in pairs, i.e., whenever two cards of the same denomination are exposed, cover them with face-up cards. Continue playing until no more plays can be made or until the entire deck is dealt out and the game is won.

Learning skills: matching
visual scanning

Poker Patience

Ages: 9 - adult

This is a challenging exercise that helps teach the rules of poker. It is almost always won.

First of all: Deal out twenty-five cards in five rows of five.

Challenge: Use the cards to create five pat poker hands of five cards each. Move as many cards as you like.

A pat hand consists of:

— a full house: three of a kind (three cards of the same denomination) plus a pair (two cards of the same denomination);
— a straight: five cards in sequence, regardless of suit. An ace may be high or low (precede a two or follow a king);
— a flush: five cards of the same suit.

Learning skills: mental flexibility
reflection
solution-searching
visual scanning
visual discrimination
matching
ordering
classification

Royal Square

Ages: 8 - adult

Object of the game: To remove all of the four middle cards in a sixteen-card layout, leaving all face cards in a prescribed layout forming a square.

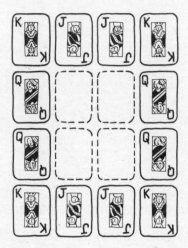

Layout: Sixteen cards are dealt out face up to form a four-by-four matrix. The layout goes as follows: first, the centre four cards are put down — that is, the second and third cards of the second and third rows. However, if a face card turns up, it is placed on the outside border of the matrix according to the following arrangement. Kings go in the corners (beginning and end of first and fourth rows). Queens go at the beginning and end of the second and third rows. Jacks are placed in the second and third slots of the first and fourth rows.

Then cards are laid out to fill in the remaining slots.

Play: When sixteen cards are laid out, cards may be removed from the layout in pairs that total 10 (6 + 4; 9 + A; two 5's; 7 + 3; 8 + 2) or a 10 may be removed by itself.

When all possible plays have been made, the empty slots needed to complete the matrix are filled from the deck. Play resumes, removing cards as before. Each time cards are dealt to the layout the four centre slots are filled in first, placing face cards in the outside slots as they turn up. If a face card cannot be placed in one of its designated slots because all are already filled, then the game is lost.

Game is won when all face cards are in their correct slot and cards have all been removed from the middle.

Strategies for play: Before placing number cards on the perimeter, consider carefully what slot you are filling. Try always to leave at least one slot for each kind of face card that may turn up, remembering always that if the face card can't be placed the game is lost.

Learning skills: addition
number facts under 10

Old Card Riddle

Why is the Shah of Persia the best Whist player in England? Because the farmers throw down their spades, the gentlemen give up their clubs, and ladies lose their hearts when they see the Shah's diamonds.

One By One

Ages: 6 - adult

This is an ancestor of Rubik's Cube and is like the square puzzles with a vacant space where printed tiles are moved one at a time until they are in numerical sequence or alphabetical order or form a picture.

First of all: Remove ace through jack of any suit. Shuffle the cards.

Layout: Deal the eleven cards face-up into four rows, with three in each of the first three rows and two in the fourth, so that the last space in the bottom row is empty.

Object of the game: To rearrange the cards so that they will be in order from ace to jack, reading left to right in each row, with ace at the upper left-hand corner and jack in the eleventh position next to the space in the lower right-hand corner.

Play: A card next to the vacant space may be moved right or down into it, leaving a vacant space. Continue rearranging cards by moving them into the space. Moves may be left or right (horizontal), up or down (vertical), but never diagonal.

Learning skills: ordering
planning
problem solving

Crossnumber Puzzle

Ages: 9 - adult

Equipment: Full deck of cards.

First of all: Remove face cards from the deck and reserve them.

Object of the game: To form a square of forty-nine cards (seven rows of seven) in which the numbers in each row and column add up to an even number. The face cards all equal zero and are used as stops like black squares in a crossword puzzle. Card values between face cards must also total an even number.

Play: Place the top card of the deck face up on the table. Deal remaining cards one at a time, placing each so that it touches a card already played. It may touch it on the top or bottom, at either side, or at one of the four corners.

Learning skills: addition
concept of odd and even numbers
planning
problem solving

Convers-a-cards — a deck by Adept/Ken Rob, Flushing, N.Y. is handy for travellers. On each card is a useful phrase written in English, Spanish, French, and German. On the four of hearts, for example, you find Where can I get a taxi? ¿Donde puedo encontrar un taxi? Ou est-ce que je peux trouver un taxi? Wo kann ich hier ein Taxi bekommen bitte?

Tower Of Hanoi

Ages: 6 - adult

First of all: Shuffle nine cards — the ace to 9 of any suit from a deck.

Layout: Make three rows of three face-up cards.

Object of the game: To move the cards until they are in one column with the 9 at the top, in descending order down to ace at the bottom.

Play: Cards are moved one at a time as follows. Only the bottom card of a column can be moved. It may be moved only to the bottom of another column and only if the card above it is of a higher denomination. When any column is completely empty the bottom card of any column may be moved to a slot at the top.

Learning skills: ordering
planning
problem solving
relative value of numbers

The oldest known deck of hand-painted playing cards dates from the late 15th century and comes from South Flanders. It was auctioned at Sotheby's in London for $143,550 — probably the most expensive deck of cards ever purchased.

Hopalong

Ages: 6 - adult

Layout: Deal out fifty face-up cards in five rows of ten each. Place a counter on the card in the upper left corner.

Object: To get the counter from the card in the upper left corner to the card in the lower right corner by moving according to a set of rules.

Play: Moves must be to a position in the same row (horizontal) or same column (vertical), alternating between jumps to cards of the same suit (from a heart to a heart) and jumps to cards of the same denomination (from a 7 to a 7).

Sample layout:

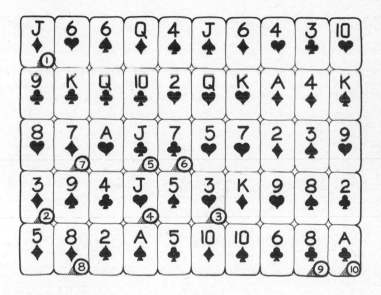

Learning skills: matching
ordering
planning
problem solving
visual-spatial concepts
right and left discrimination

GAMES

Fifty-two Pick-Up

Ages: 5 - 12

Warning to all adults: If a child suggests you play this game, refuse politely.

This is not a real game, but a time-honoured part of the culture of childhood. It seems to be passed on by children to children, usually slightly younger — almost as part of an initiation to the world of card-playing. One child says to the other, "Do you want to play Fifty-two Pick-up?" The unsuspecting victim indicates his willingness. Then the initiator takes a deck of cards, throws them in the air, points to the cards scattered on the floor, and says, "Fifty-two pick-up!"

Having been fooled, the child can hardly wait to find his own victim.

Learning skills: none whatsoever

Knuckles

Ages: 6 - 12   **Players:** 2

Sara, eleven, taught me this game. She said that a player could rap the table with her knuckles if she thought she had the lower score. Both players show their hands; the one with the lower score wins.

Object of the game: To end up with the cards totalling the lowest possible value.

Equipment: A deck of cards.

Value of cards: Cards 2 to 10 are equal to their face value; ace = 1; jack = 0; queen and king = 10.

First of all: Dealer deals a hand of 5 cards to each player and places the rest of the deck face down in the middle.

Play: First player takes the top card of the pack and may exchange it for any card in his hand. He does this only if it is lower than one of the cards. The discarded card is placed face up beside the face-down pack. Next player may take the face-up card or pick the top card of the pack and either change it for a card in his hand or discard it. Play continues, with players changing cards in their hands for lower ones until all the cards in the pack have been picked. The player with the lowest cards is the winner. The winner is, invariably, the one with the most jacks and aces.

Learning skills: concepts of "higher" and "lower"
                     addition

Big Bango

Ages: 3 - adult   **Players:** any number

This is a variation of Bango, which uses five cards. Big Bango uses nine, sixteen, or twenty-five cards, and was sent to me by Elizabeth Lohman, director of the Learning Center in Wayne, Pennsylvania.

Object of the game: To be the first one to cover all the cards.

Equipment: A deck of cards for each player and one for the dealer. (If some of the children don't know card names, it is nice if the dealer has a jumbo-size deck of cards so that everyone can see the card as the dealer calls its name.)

First of all: Each child deals his own hand — a face-up grid of 25 cards (5 rows of 5). A grid of nine cards (3 rows of 3) or sixteen cards (4 rows of 4) may also be used.

Play: Dealer takes the full deck and turns up cards one at a time, naming each one aloud. If a player has a card that is called, he covers it with a face-down card from his deck. When all his cards are covered, he calls "Bango".

Learning skills: careful listening
visual scanning of array
multiplication, e.g.: $5 \times 5 = 25$

Bichos

Ages: 5 - 12   **Players:** 3 - 10

Children in Portugal play this game; "bichos" means "animals".

Object of the game: To be the first to get rid of all your cards.

Equipment: One, two, or three decks of cards, depending on the number of players (one deck for three or four; two decks for five or six; three decks for larger groups.)

First of all: Shuffle decks together and deal out all cards in face-down stacks in front of the players. Each player chooses the name of an animal and announces it. Other players must remember each player's "animal" and use it in the game.

Play: All players simultaneously turn up the top card of their stack. If a player's card matches, in denomination, any other player's card, he calls out that player's "animal". The last player to call the animal correctly must take in the matching cards and add them to his stack. If there are no matches, the cards remain face up in front of the players and new cards are played on the face-up pile. At the next match, the loser takes in all the cards in the face-up pile. If there are three-way matches, and one player correctly calls out the names of the two players before his is called out, then the losers divide up the winner's cards. Play continues until one player has no cards left and is the winner.

Tips for good play: *Children in Portugal try to choose strange animal names that their opponents will find hard to remember — not just dog, cat, and horse, but names like orangutan, rhinoceros, and chinchilla.*

Variation: Choose names from other semantic domains, e.g. vegetables, furniture, diseases. Switch categories from time to time during play to keep players on their toes.

Learning skills: visual scanning
fast visual responses
practice in visual discrimination
rapid word retrieval

Paul's Game

Ages: 4 - 12   **Players:** 2

Paul answered questions monosyllabically and volunteered nothing when he came to see me for testing — until I pulled out a deck of cards. Then his eyes lit up, he became more cheerful and animated. It was much easier for him to take tests and expose some of his disabilities after he had had the opportunity to reveal his strengths — good card sense, fast visual reactions, incredible memory, and an impressive repertoire of games. This is one of them.

Object of the game: To be able to play a card of the same suit as a face-up card — either from the table or from your hand.

Equipment: A deck of cards.

First of all: Deal all of the cards face down in rows on the table.

Play: Each player turns over a card, leaving it in place. He must then find a card of the same suit. He turns over cards one at a time, taking them into his hand if they are not of the suit he is looking for. As soon as he gets a card of the needed suit, he puts it on the turned-up card, then covers it with a face-up card of a different suit from his hand. (Should the same-suit card be found on the first try and the player does not yet have cards in his hand, he must keep turning over cards to get one of a different suit. Until he gets one, all other cards are taken into his hand.)

The next player turns up cards one at a time until he finds one of the same suit as the new face-up card. As before, he takes all the others into his hand. When he gets a card of the right suit, he puts it on the pile and covers it with a face-up card from his hand — of a different suit from the one just played. The play continues, with players following suit from the cards in their hand or turning up cards from the table until they get one. When all the cards on the table have been turned over and one player cannot follow suit, that player is the loser.

Learning skills: visual matching

Finders Keepers

Age: 5 - adult   **Players:** 2 - 4

Object of the game: Players take in cards that total a predetermined sum.

Equipment: A deck of cards.

Value of cards: Ace = 1; two = 2 through ten = 10; jack = 11; queen = 12; king = 13. For younger children with limited computational skills I sometimes let all face cards equal 10.

First of all: Lay out all the cards face down in 6 rows of 8, with a 7th row of 4 cards.

Play: First player names a number and then turns up any two cards. If the cards total that number he takes in both cards. If not, one card is left face-up, the other is turned over again in its original place.

The next player then turns up two cards and sees if he can make the predetermined sum with two or more of the face-up cards. If he is successful, he takes in the cards. If not, he leaves one face-up and turns over the other(s).

When a player succeeds in making the total, he chooses the next number that will be the sum the players try to make.

The winner is the player who has the most cards when all the cards are turned up.

Tips for good play:
1. *Try to remember the value and location of some of the cards that have been turned over and replaced. Knowing where a particular number is located allows a player to go directly to the card needed to complete a total.*
2. *After your turn, think carefully about which card you will leave face up. You may be able to make it harder for the next player to get the cards that will equal the total he is after.*

Learning skills: addition
              visual-spatial concepts

Asa Pilia Tutto

Ages: 5 - 14   **Players:** 2 - 5

A variation of "Steal the Pack", taught to me by Franco, 14; it means Ace Takes All.

Object of the game: To get the most cards by taking in cards from the table, or the opponent's stack, with a matching card.

Equipment: A deck of cards.

First of all: Deal three cards to each player and four face-up cards in the middle.

Play: Non-dealer goes first, playing a card. If the card has the same face value as any card on the table, the cards are taken in. Taken-in cards are placed in a face-up pile in front of the player who earned them. If player has no match, a card is played to the table.

Players play in turn, playing a card to the table, or taking in a match, or, best of all, stealing an opponent's pile with a card that matches the top face-up card or any ace.

After each hand of three cards is played out, three more cards are dealt. When all the cards in the deck have been played, players count their cards. The player with the most cards is the winner.

Learning skills: matching
              visual scanning

Mariage

Ages: 4 - 12   **Players:** 3

Benoit, a teen-aged summer visitor from France, taught us his country's version of a familiar North American game. The French title means wedding.

Object of the game: To avoid holding the key card at the end.

Equipment: A deck of cards.

First of all: Dealer chooses the key card, and removes the same colour card of that denomination from the deck. Other players do not know which card has been chosen. The entire deck is dealt out.

Play: Players remove from hand pairs of cards of the same colour and denomination (e.g. 4 of hearts, 4 of diamonds).

When all pairs have been removed, each player in turn may pick a card from the hand of the player to his right. As the same colour pairs are formed, they are removed from the hand. The player left with the key card is the loser. ("Pas de mariage", said Benoit, which means "no wedding".)

Learning skills: matching (colour and number)

The total different sequences possible in a 52 card deck is a figure 68 numerals long.

It is said that the four suit symbols originally represented the four classes in the society of medieval Europe. Clubs represented the peasants and serfs, diamonds the merchants, hearts the clergy, and spades the nobles. This ranking of suits still holds in "Bridge".

Jackass

Ages: 4 - 10   **Players:** 2 - 8

This is the version of "Old Maid" that is played in Trinidad. In this West Indian version, it is the "male" card that is to be avoided.

Object of the game: To avoid being left with the odd jack.

Equipment: A deck of cards.

First of all: Remove the jack of diamonds from the deck and play with a deck of 51 cards. Deal out all the cards, one at a time, to the players.

Play: Players make pairs of all cards of the same denomination in their hands (e.g. two 2's, two queens) and put them aside. Each player in turn, without looking at the cards, may pick one card from the hand of the player to his right. If it is the same denomination as any card in his hand, he forms a pair and puts it aside. If not, he adds the card to his hand. Play continues until all cards have been paired off and one player, left with the single jack, is declared the Jackass.

Learning skills: matching (numbers)

Suck The Well

Ages: 5 - 14   **Players:** 2 - 4

With three or four players this game has more suspense, more excitement, because you are never sure who is going to win the pile. This particular version comes from Barbados.

Object of the game: To win all the cards by turning up high cards.

Equipment: A deck of cards.

First of all: For authentic Caribbean play, deal anticlockwise, from right to left. Deck is dealt out equally among all the players. Players keep their cards in a face-down pile in front of them.

Play: Player to the dealer's right begins, and play continues to the right. Cards are faced up by each player in turn, one at a time, on a pile in the centre. Player who plays a "royal" — a face card or an ace — is eligible to take in the pile. But first, the player next in line must "pay" him by playing cards on his.

On a jack — one card
On a queen — two cards
On a king — three cards
On an ace — four cards

However, if, while "paying", player turns up a "royal", then payment stops and the next player must begin payment according to the above values. If none of the payment cards is a "royal", then the player who played the last "royal" takes in all the cards in the pile, putting them on the bottom of his own stack. The player who took in the cards plays the next card. If a player has no more cards, he drops out of the game and play continues among remaining players. The player to get all the cards is the winner.

Learning skills: counting
distinguishing among face cards and responding
appropriately

Ronda Robada

Ages: 5 - 12   **Players:** 2 - 4

Object of the game: To get the most cards.

Equipment: A deck of cards.

First of all: Deal four face-up cards to the middle of the table and three cards to each player.

Play: First player may take in a card from the table with a card of the same denomination. Then he may pick up from the table any card higher or lower in sequence to the "matched" cards (regardless of suit), continuing to take in any card one higher or lower than the last card taken. Cards taken in are placed in a face-up stack in front of the players.

Subsequent players take in cards the same way. Any player, at his turn, may take in an opponent's stack if he has a card that matches or is one higher or lower than the top card of the stack. When the first three cards are played out, three more cards are dealt to each player. Play continues until all cards are dealt out. Player with the most cards at that time is the winner.

Learning skills: numerical ordering — forwards and backwards
visual scanning
matching

Speed

Ages: 6 - adult   **Players:** 2

This is a logical name for the frenzied race between two players to get their cards on the table.

Equipment: A deck of cards.

First of all: Deal two face-down piles of four cards each, one to the right of each player. These are the starter cards. The rest of the deck is dealt out so that each player has a face-down pack. Players take the top four cards of their face-down piles as a hand, replacing cards as they are played so that they always hold a four-card hand.

Play: Players simultaneously turn up the top card of the starter cards to their right, placing the cards face up in the middle of the table so that there are two cards side by side. These are the cards to be played on.

Players now, as fast as they can (with no regard for taking turns) try to play cards from their hands on the face-up piles. A card may be played, regardless of suit, if it is one more or one less than the card on top of the pile. Thus, on a 7 a player may play a 6 or an 8. On a king, a player may play a queen or an ace. As plays are made, players may take cards from their face-down stack, always keeping four cards in their hands.

When no more plays can be made, players, again simultaneously, turn up the top card from the piles on their right onto the face-up playing piles, and play resumes. When the four-card stack is used up, the face-up stacks are turned over to replace the stacks at the right. These are used to provide the starter cards. Play continues until one player gets rid of all his cards and is the winner.

Learning skills: visual scanning
fast visual-motor responses
moving up and down the number line

Piri Picciu

Ages: 5 - adult   **Players:** 4

Object of the game: To get rid of all your cards.

Equipment: Deck of forty Italian cards or an ordinary deck with face cards removed.

First of all: Deal ten cards to each player. Cards are kept in a face-down pile in front of each player.

Play: First player turns up a card. If it is an ace it goes in the centre, to be built up on in sequence, according to suit. Otherwise, it is put face up in front of the player. Next player turns up a card. It may be played to the centre if an ace or next in suit to an ace already played. If it is one higher or lower than an opponent's face-up card (regardless of suit), it may be placed on the opponent's pile. Otherwise, it goes face up in front of the players.

Play continues this way, with players playing to the centre, if possible — an ace, or in suit sequence on the ace piles, or on any player's face-up pile. When face-down piles are used up, players turn over their face-up piles. Play continues until one player has no more cards and is the winner.

Learning skills: practice in categorizing and arranging numbers in
                        sequence
                        visual scanning

Switch

Ages: 5 - 12   **Players:** 2 - 6

There seems to be some version of "Crazy Eights" everywhere in the world. This version is played in Brisbane, Australia.

Object of the game: To be the first to get rid of all your cards.

Equipment: A deck of cards.

First of all: Deal eight cards to each player. Place the rest of the deck in the middle. Turn up the top card of the deck and place it beside the deck.

Play: Players in turn must play a card to the turned up pile. It may be a card of the same suit as the top card, or of the same denomination. However, if an ace is played, play is switched to any suit player names.

The first player to get rid of all the cards is the winner of the hand. Cards left in the losers' hands are added up and count against them. Cards equal face value; face cards count 10 points each.

Cards are shuffled and redealt until one player's score reaches a predetermined number, (e.g. 100) and is the loser.

Learning skills: set-changing
matching
classification
addition

Happy Birthday

Ages: 5 - 12   **Players:** 2 - 4

I invented this game for the many children who have specific trouble learning ordered lists. They need more repetition than their peers. The challenge is to find opportunities to rehearse the lists and to make the repetition palatable.

Object of the game: To follow in sequence the recitation of months by playing a card next in numerical sequence regardless of suit; to win points by playing the card that represents your own birthday month; to be the first player to get rid of all your cards.

Equipment: One deck of cards with kings removed.

Value of cards: Cards (ace to queen) represent months of the year, with ace = January, 2 = February, through to Jack = November, Queen = December.

First of all: Each player tells the month of his or her birthday. Deal out all the cards.

Play: Player to dealer's left may begin if he has an ace. If he cannot play, play passes to the left. The first player to play an ace says "January". Next player plays any 2 (or passes to the first player in line who has one). Player playing the 2 says "February". And so on, in sequence, to Queen—December. Next player plays an ace and says "January". If a player plays the card that stands for his birthday month, he automatically gets twelve points. All players, without being reminded, must say "Happy Birthday". The first one to say it gets points equivalent to the card played (one point for an ace, two for a 2, etc.).

If a player has no more cards he goes out of the game. If he is the first to do so he gets points equivalent to four times the value of the last card he played. If he is second to go out he gets points equivalent to three times the value of the last card played. If third, he gets points equivalent to twice the value of the card he played. There are no points for being last to go out. Play continues until the months have been recited four times.

Learning skills: memorizing the months of the year in order
                       learning the numerical position of the months
                       hanging on to arbitrary pieces of information
                       keeping several variables in mind
                       staying alert
                       multiplying by 2, 3, and 4

Creights

Ages: 6 - adult   **Players:** 3 - 6

There are more rules to remember in this game than "Crazy Eights" yet all children seem to be able to retain the complex inventory of card values and procedures. This game promotes lots of arithmetic practice.

Object of the game: To get rid of all your cards by playing a card that matches (according to a set of rules) the card that is face up in the centre of the table.

Equipment: For three or four players, use one deck of 52 cards; for more, use two decks shuffled together.

First of all: There are fifteen hands to a game. The number of cards dealt to each player changes with each hand, as follows:

Hand 1 — 8 cards	Hand 9 — 2 cards
Hand 2 — 7 cards	Hand 10 — 3 cards
Hand 3 — 6 cards	Hand 11 — 4 cards
Hand 4 — 5 cards	Hand 12 — 5 cards
Hand 5 — 4 cards	Hand 13 — 6 cards
Hand 6 — 3 cards	Hand 14 — 7 cards
Hand 7 — 2 cards	Hand 15 — 8 cards
Hand 8 — 1 cards	

After the cards have been dealt, the remainder of the deck is placed face down in the centre of the table. The top card is turned up beside it.

Wild cards are 8's and 9's.

Play: Players, at their turn, must play a card from their hands face up on top of the face-up pile. As in "Crazy Eights", it must match the face-up card in suit or in denomination, or it may be a "wild" card. For example, if the face-up card is the three of clubs, player may play any club, any 3, or any 8 or 9. If a player cannot make a play he must take a card from the top of the deck. Play then passes to the left.

The card on top of the face-up pile may change the order of play according to the following rules:

4 — skip one player;

5 — all players take a card;

6 — player who played it must go again (and must play a card matching in suit or denomination or a wild card);

7 — player second from the left of the player who played it must draw a face-down card; otherwise play continues normally;

8 — player who played it can name the suit the next player must match;

9 — player who played it must name a suit different in colour from the 9 just played. That becomes the suit for next player to match;

10 — play changes direction, so that next play is made by player to the right. Play continues counterclockwise until the next 10 is played.

Special rules for 2's and aces: When a two is played, each player who follows must play either an ace or a 2. A wild card is not permissible. When the first 2 is played, a count begins. Players count 1 for each ace, 2 for each 2. If a player is unable to play an ace or a 2, he must add to his hand as many cards from the deck as the number of the count. Play passes to the next player, who plays normally — either a card of the same suit or rank as the last card played, or a wild card. When the next 2 is played, the count is started again.

Play continues until one player "goes out" — gets rid of all his cards. If, before this happens, the face-down deck is used up, the player whose turn it is to draw shuffles the face-up pile — leaving the face-up card that determines his play — and places it face down. Players are penalized for each shuffle that takes place at their turn.

Going out: On the turn before a player goes out, he must announce to the other players that he has only one card left. If he fails to notify his opponents, then he is not allowed to go out, but instead must draw two cards from the deck. When a player does go out, the round does not end until the other players have responded to the card played. If the card played is a 6, player must go again and therefore must draw cards. If he is not able to play the first card he draws, he will not be able to go out. Similarly, if his last card is a 2, players are obliged to begin counting and playing 2's or aces in turn. If his turn comes round while the count is still taking place, then he will have to draw the requisite amount of cards and will be unable to go out.

Scoring: After a player goes out, players add up the points in the cards they are left with according to the following rules:

Ace	1 point
2	20 points
3	Each 3 changes the scoring value of one other card in the hand to 3. Only 8's are exempt.
4	15
5	30
6	30
7	25
8	50
9	50
10	25
Jack	10
Queen	10
King	10

Shuffling penalty — for a player's first shuffle of the game — 5 points. For each subsequent shuffle of the game (even in a new hand) the penalty is doubled — 10 for the second, 20 for the third, etc.

Winner is the player with the lowest score at the end of 15 rounds.

Learning skills: mental flexibility
memory skills
right and left discrimination
matching
classification

Ciao Seppe

Ages: 5 - 12   **Players:** 2 - 5

"Ciao" is an Italian greeting like "Hi" or "So long", and "Seppe" is short for Guiseppe; it is pronounced Chow Sepp and a translation might be "So long, Joe". Despite its title, this game is played in Switzerland, and is another version of "Crazy Eights".

Object of the game: To get rid of all your cards.

Equipment: In Switzerland, this is played with a forty-card deck (no 2's, 3's, 4's, or 5's), but a deck of 52 will do.

First of all: Deal nine cards to each player. Put the deck in the middle and turn up the top card.

Play: For authentic Swiss play, play is counterclockwise. Player to the dealer's right goes first and turns pass to the right. Players, at their turn, must play a card of the same suit or the same denomination as the face-up card, unless they have a jack. A jack can change the suit to any suit the player names. Playing a 9 allows a player to play two cards (both must follow the rule of same suit or denomination). Playing an 8 causes the next player to miss a turn.

First player to go out says "Ciao Seppe" and is the winner.

Learning skills: classification
matching
mental flexibility

Jacks Wild

Ages: 5 - 14   **Players:** 3

Kirsten, age 13 taught me this German version of "Crazy Eights".

Equipment: Deck of 52 cards

Object of the game: To be the first to get rid of your cards.

Value of cards: In scoring, at the end of the hand, face cards are equal to 10; all other cards are equal to their denominational value.

First of all: Deal 7 cards to each player. Place the deck in the middle and turn up the top card.

Play: Player to the dealer's left may play, onto the face-up card, a card of the same suit or denomination. If there is no possible play, then player must take the top card from the deck. Play passes to the left. Players, in turn must play a card onto the last card played, either of the same suit or denomination, or pick a card.

Special Rules: If an 8 is played — or is the first card faced-up — the next player misses a turn, unless that player can play an 8 which cancels the first 8. Then the following player must miss a turn.

If a 7 is faced-up, the next player must pick up 2 cards, unless a 7 is played on it. Following a second 7 the next player must pick up 4 cards.

Jacks are wild. A Jack can be played on any card and player may name the suit it stands for. A Jack cannot cancel a 7.

Play continues until one player has no more cards and is the winner of the hand. Other players total the value of the cards remaining in their hands. If a Jack was the last card played, the other players double the value of the cards in their hand. The winner of the game is the player who has the lowest score after an agreed on number of hands.

Learning skills: matching
classification
memory development
mental flexibility

Xeri

Ages: 6 - adult   **Players:** 2 or 2 teams of 2

This game that Greek children play, has echoes of "Casino", the game I played most as a young child.

Equipment: Deck of 52 cards.

Object of the game: To earn points by taking in key cards

Value of cards: Cards are not ranked in play, but jacks are "wild" and can be used as a match for any card.

Cards taken in have the following point value: jack, queen, king, ace = 1 point each
10 of diamonds = 2 points
2 of clubs = 2 points
Each Xeri = 10 points

First of all: Deal 6 cards to each player and four overlapping face-up cards on the table.

Play: Non-dealer goes first. Players take turns playing a card from their hand to the top of the face-up stack. If player has a card in hand of the same denomination as the card on the top of the stack, or a jack, player takes in the stack. Cards taken in are kept in a face down stack in front of the player.

If there is only one card on the table and a player takes it in, it is faced up in the player's stack as a Xeri. Each Xeri counts as 10 points when points are totalled.

After the six cards have been played six more are dealt. Play continues until all cards are dealt and played. Then players' scores are totalled.

Game continues with dealers alternating until one player has 100 points and is the winner.

Learning skills: matching
addition
remembering key cards

Spoof

Ages: 5 - adult   **Players:** 2 or more

This game is also known as "Drop 7" but I remember it as "Fan Tan" which I played as a child in Nova Scotia. In this version, the order of the suits is prescribed.

Object of the game: To get rid of all the cards.

Equipment: A deck of cards.

First of all: All of the cards are dealt out.

Play: Each player is allowed to play one card. Player to dealer's right goes first, then each player in turn. To start the play, player must have the 7 of diamonds. Player must pass if he cannot put down that card. First player to have it places it on the table.

Players, in turn, may play the 7 of clubs or the diamond card that follows or precedes the 7, placing the 6 on one side of the 7 and the 8 on the other side. Subsequent players may continue to place cards in sequence, building either up (on the 8) or down (on the 6), or they may play a 7. The 7 of hearts may be played only after the 7 of clubs has been played, and the 7 of spades only after the 7 of hearts. Players *must* play a card if they have a play. Otherwise, they pass. Play continues until one player gets rid of all his cards and is the winner.

Strategies: *If you have a choice of plays, choose the one most likely to prevent your opponent from going out. For example, if you suspect he has the ace of hearts and you have the two, you will hold it back so that he is unable to play that card.*

Learning skills: remembering order of suits to be played
(diamonds, clubs, hearts, spades)
numerical ordering (forwards and backwards)

King's Market

Ages: 5 - adult   **Players:** 2 - 8

Object of the game: To play the key queen and so take the money on the designated king, and to be the first to get rid of one's cards.

Equipment: A deck of cards; chips or tokens.

First of all: Put four kings in the middle. Players choose one of the kings to be the key card. Each player puts a chip on that king and one chip in the middle.

Deal out the whole pack, creating one extra hand. Dealer, if he doesn't like his own hand, can change it for the spare hand. If he does not want the spare hand, the next player can buy it, paying the dealer one chip.

Play: Whoever has the ace of spades plays first and plays that card (or if there is no ace of spades, then the player who has the lowest spade plays it). Player who has the next card in that suit plays. If no one can play, because the next card is not available, the player who played the last card must play the lowest red card in his hand. Players follow suit in sequence until that suit is stopped. Next player to play a card must play her lowest black card. The player who plays the queen of the same suit as the king with the money on it takes the money.

The player to get rid of all his cards first is the winner and takes the money in the middle. If the money on the king is not claimed, then it stays for the next turn.

Learning skills: concepts of "lowest" and "highest"
numerical ordering

New Market

Ages: 6 - adult   **Players:** 3 - 5

Object of the game: To be first to get rid of all your cards.

Equipment: Deck of 52 cards plus ace of spades, king of hearts, queen of clubs, jack of diamonds taken from another deck. These are "boodle" cards. Chips or counters.

First of all: Place the boodle cards face up on the table. Each player puts one chip on each boodle card.

Deal: 6 cards each to 5 players
       7 cards each to 4 players
       8 cards each to 3 players
An extra hand is dealt to the left of the dealer face down so no one sees it.

Play: First player leads the lowest card of any suit in his hand. Next player must play next highest card of same suit (if first player played a 7 of spades, this player must play the 8). If he cannot play, the turn passes to the next player. Players continue to play until the suit is stopped (no one can continue in sequence). Last player who put down a card plays the lowest card in his hand of a new suit. If he has only cards in the stopped suit, the play passes to the left.

Whoever plays a card identical to a boodle card takes the chips on that boodle.

First player out of cards gets one chip from each of the other players.

Leftover boodle chips are saved for the next round.

Learning skills: numerical ordering
                  classification
                  concept of "lowest"
                  matching

King's Corner

Ages: 6 - Adult   **Players:** 2

I first played this game on a Caribbean Island. I learned it from a 10 year old, and it is undoubtedly a children's game but I enjoyed playing it so much that I have indicated its suitability for a wide age range. I find it has much of the appeal of a Solitaire. Players have to stay alert and scan the layout for possible plays.

Object of the game: To get rid of cards in the hand by playing them on the layout.

First of all: Remove the four kings from the deck and lay them face up to form four diagonal corners for a layout which will have four more face up cards.

Deal: Deal four face up cards, placing each between two kings, to form the layout. Deal eight cards to each player. The deck is placed in the middle.

Play: Players take turns. At each turn player draws a card from the top of the deck and may play cards onto the layout. A card may be played if it is opposite in colour and one lower in value than a top face-up card. (Thus, a red nine is played on a black ten; a black queen on a red king, etc.). During a turn a player may make all possible plays. If any of the cards in the layout itself can be placed on another one, player may do so, filling the empty space with a card from his hand. Play continues until one player has no more cards and is the winner.

Learning skills: numerical ordering
principle of alternation
visual scanning

Odds And Evens

Ages: 6 - 12   **Players:** 2

This game was created by a psychologist colleague of mine, Sylvia Rid-dell, as an imaginative approach to understanding the concept of odd and even numbers.

Object of the game: To win all the cards.

Equipment: One deck of cards.

Value of cards: Ace − 10 = face value; jack = 11; queen = 12; king = 13.

First of all: One player picks a card. If it is an odd number, he is designated "Odd" and his opponent "Even." If it is an even number, the situation is reversed. Deal out all the cards so that each player has half the deck in a face-down pile.

Play: Players simultaneously turn up the top card of their packs. They add the numerical values of the two cards. If the total is odd, "Odd" takes it in and vice versa. Cards taken in are placed at the bottom of the player's pack. Play continues until one player wins all the cards.

Learning skills: addition

understanding the concept of odd and even numbers (not divisible by 2 and divisible by 2)

There is an inn in Devonshire, England called the Pack o' Cards Inn. It was built in the 17th century to celebrate the owner's luck at gambling. The inn has four floors, 52 windows, and 13 doors.

Hockey

Ages: 6 - adult   **Players:** 2

After a summer of French immersion in Trois Rivières, my daughter brought back this game — as well as language facility. This game must have originated in Quebec, and is the only truly Canadian card game I know.

Object of the game: To win the most goals in three periods. A period consists of all the hands played in one deck.

First of all: Dealer decides the number of cards he will deal in each hand, and deals the same number to himself and to his opponent.

Play: First player plays a card face up to the centre of the table. The next player partially covers it with a face-up card from his hand. If the card is of the same denomination (say, 2 on a 2), it constitutes a pass. Two passes on two consecutive turns constitute a goal. So, for example, if player A plays a 3 and player B follows with a 3, that constitutes a pass. If player A then plays another 3, he scores a goal. However, if player B plays the fourth card of the denomination, the goal is nullified — and becomes *no goal*.

A jack is an automatic pass. If a player plays a jack on an immediately previous jack, he scores a goal. This can, of course, be cancelled by a third jack. But the fourth jack played on that one will call back the goal.

When the cards are played out, dealer deals another hand from the remaining cards and the play continues. Hands are dealt out until the deck is finished. This marks the end of the first period.

The deal changes hands for the second period, and then changes back for the third. If the score is tied at the end of three periods, the game goes into "sudden death" overtime; the first player to score wins.

Learning skills: matching
                 the vocabulary of hockey

Donkey

Ages: 5 - 12   **Players:** 2 - 4

Object of the game: To be first to get rid of your cards.

First of All: Deal seven cards to each player. Put the remainder of the deck in the middle. Turn up the top card of the deck and leave it face up beside the deck. This card determines the first suit to be played.

Play: Player to the dealer's left must play a card of the turned-up suit. If he doesn't have it he keeps drawing cards from the deck until he can play one of that suit. The next player follows suit. (If he can't, he turns up cards until he gets a playable one.) The one who plays the highest card is considered the winner of the trick. Winner takes in the cards and puts them aside, then "leads" to the next play. Player who leads can play a card of any suit and other players must follow suit. If they cannot, they keep drawing cards until they can. Play continues as above.

When the deck is exhausted, play continues from the hand. If a player plays a suit and no one has cards to follow suit, he plays all the cards of that suit in his hand, and then plays a card of another suit. The first player to get rid of all his cards is the winner. Play can then continue among remaining players. The last one with cards in his hand is the Donkey. The number of cards in his hand tells what age donkey he is, e.g. two cards signify a two-year-old donkey.

Learning skills: classification
relational value of numbers ("higher", "lower", "highest", etc.)

Go To Pack

Ages: 5 - 12   **Players:** 2 or more

This game is a version of "Donkey" and both games are played in the Caribbean.

Object of the game: To be the first to get rid of your cards.

First of all: Players decide on the penalty for each card remaining in the loser's hand. The Barbadian children with whom I played used penalties such as number of glasses of water to be drunk, number of times to do the dishes.

Deal three or four cards to each player. Put the pack in the middle. Turn up the top card. This determines the suit to be played.

Play: First player must play a card following suit of the turned-up card. If he can't, he "goes to pack", picking up cards one at a time until he can play. Other players do the same. The player of the highest card takes in the pile and makes the next play. The card he plays determines the suit of the next round. The play continues in this way until there are no more cards in the pack.

When there are no more cards in the pack and player cannot follow suit, he picks up the card and his opponent gives him a card to play.

The first player to get rid of all his cards is the winner. Each card remaining in the loser's hand determines how many penalties he pays. With four cards left over, he may have to drink four cups of water.

Tips for good play:
1. *Try to play high cards in order to be the one to decide what suit is played.*
2. *Try to keep track of suits that have been played and of how many cards in that suit have been played. This will give you an idea of what suits remain in your opponent's hand.*

Learning skills: classification
　　　　　　　　　relational value of numbers ("higher", "lower", "highest", etc.)

Burro Empé

Ages: 5 - 12   **Players:** 2 - 4

In Portugal, "Donkey" is known as "Burro Deitado" or "Lying Donkey". This is a version of that game, and only differs in the placement of the deck on the table. Its title translates as "Standing Donkey".

Object of the game: To be the first to get rid of all your cards by following suit.

First of all: Deal four cards to each player. The remaining deck is divided in half and the two halves are placed in standing position — to form a tent-like structure — with backs facing outward.

Play: First player (to the dealer's right, in Portugal) plays any card. Players, in turn, must follow suit. If a player cannot follow suit, he must pick a card from the stack. He tries to do this as carefully as possible so that the stack remains standing. He must take as many cards as adhere to the card he is trying to remove; or, if he knocks down the stack, he takes the entire stack. Player keeps drawing cards until he can follow suit. The player who played the highest card takes in the cards and puts them aside. He leads to the next trick. When the deck is exhausted, play continues from the hand. If a player plays a suit and none of the others can follow suit, the player who led it plays all of the cards of that suit that are in his hands, and then leads a card of another suit. Play continues until one player gets rid of all the cards in his hand and is the winner.

Penalty: If a player is caught deliberately shaking the table while an opponent is drawing a card, then the player must draw two cards.

Learning skills: fine motor dexterity
                classification
                relational value of numbers ("higher", "lower", "highest", etc.)

Fallout

Ages: 6 - adult   **Players:** 4 - 6

Object of the game: To take in tricks so that you can add to your hand from the stack and be the only player in the game with cards remaining.

Equipment: A deck of cards; chips or tokens.

Value of the cards: From lowest to highest: 2, 3, 4, 5, 6, 7, 8, 9, 10, J, Q, K, A.

First of all: Cut the cards to determine trump. Each player puts a chip in the pot. Deal four cards each to four players; five cards each to five players; six cards each to six players. Place deck in the centre of the table.

Play: Player to the dealer's left leads. Players follow suit in turn if they can. If a player cannot follow suit, he may play a trump or any card from another suit. If no trump card has been played, highest card of suit led takes in the trick. Otherwise, highest trump takes in the trick. Winner of the trick picks the top card of the deck and leads to the next trick. Play continues. When a player has no more cards, he withdraws from the game. Last player left holding cards is the winner and takes in the pot.

Before each new hand the deck is shuffled, cards are cut to determine trump, and each player puts a chip in the pot.

Learning skills: classification (following suit)
number values

King

Ages: 6 - adult   **Players:** 4

"King", played by children in Portugal, is really six different games played in sequence. Each is a nice little game in its own right. When played as a mega-game, the rules change with each new hand. Players must continually change their set and remember the objectives of the current hand.

Object of the game: To win or to avoid tricks, to win or to avoid key cards, depending on which hand in the sequence is being played.

The game consists of twelve hands. The first six are "positive", where players get credit for key cards; the next six are "negative", where players lose points for key cards.

First of all: Players draw cards to determine dealer. They keep drawing until one gets a king and is the dealer of the first hand. After that, deal passes to the right.

All of the cards are dealt out. Dealer, after looking at his cards, names trump (the suit that will rank the highest for this hand) or decides that there will be no trump.

Play: Player to the dealer's right plays the first card. All players must follow suit if they can. Highest card takes in the trick. If a player cannot

follow suit, a trump card may be played and a trump card outranks any other card. In the case of two trump cards, the higher trump wins the trick.

Rules for individual hands:
"Positives": the object of the game is to take in cards or tricks.
Game 1: As many tricks as possible. Score 25 for each trick taken.
Game 2: Hearts. Each heart scores 20 points.
Game 3: Women (queens). Score 50 points for each.
Game 4: Men (kings and jacks). Score 30 points for each.
Game 5: King of hearts. Score 150 points.
Game 6: Last two tricks. Score 100 for the next-to-last trick, 150 for the last trick.
"Negatives": the object of the game is to avoid tricks or cards.
Game 7: Tricks. Lose 25 points for each trick taken.
Game 8: Hearts. Lose 20 points for each heart taken.
Game 9: Women. Lose 50 points for each queen taken.
Game 10: Men. Lose 30 points for each king or jack taken.
Game 11: King of hearts. Lose 150 points if this card is taken.
Game 12: Last two tricks: lose 100 points if the next-to-last trick is taken, lose 150 points if the last trick is taken.

Winner is the player with the highest score at the end of twelve hands.

Learning skills: mental flexibility
memory skills
classification
relational value of numbers ("higher", "lower", "highest", etc.)
addition
subtraction

Nine To Zero

Ages: 8 - adult   **Players:** 3

Object of the game: To be the first to reduce one's score from 9 to 0 by taking in tricks.

Equipment: A deck of cards.

Value of cards: Cards are equal to face value. Trumps are higher than any other suit. Trump suit changes with each hand, starting with hearts, then diamonds, spades, clubs, and finally no trump.

First of all: Players each pick a card to determine the dealer. Lowest card deals. Deal then passes to the left. Players each start with a score of 9. Dealer deals four hands of thirteen cards each, one hand to each player and one as a "dummy".

Play: Player on dealer's left may trade his hand for the dummy hand. If he does not want it, next player may trade, and if no trade is made, the next player has the option.

Player at dealer's left leads to the first trick. Players must follow suit, or if they cannot follow suit, they may trump or discard any card. Highest card played takes in the trick. Player who takes in the trick leads to the next trick.

Scoring: A player must take in four tricks to break even. For every trick less than four a point is added to player's score. For every trick over four a point is subtracted from player's score. After each hand is played out, cards are shuffled and redealt until one player reaches zero and is the winner.

Learning skills: subtraction
classification

Nine-Five-Two

Ages: 8 - adult   **Players:** 3

Object of the game: To make the designated number of tricks in each hand and be the first to achieve a score of 0.

First of all: Each player picks a card to determine the number of tricks he must make. If two players pick cards of the same denomination, they pick again. The holder of the highest card must make nine tricks, the middle card five tricks, and the lowest card two tricks. The holder of the highest card is the dealer. Aces are the highest cards.

The entire deck is dealt to the three players, except for the last four cards, which are placed face down at the side. The dealer, after inspecting his cards, may choose to discard four and take the four face-down cards.

Play: Player to the dealer's left plays any card. Other players must follow suit. Highest card takes in the trick and leads to the next trick. If a player cannot follow suit he can play any card. Play continues until all cards have been played. Players count their tricks.

Scoring: Each player begins with a score of 9. The first person to get 0 is the winner. If a player makes his designated number of tricks, his score stays the same. For every trick over, he loses a point. For every trick under he gains a point. (For every player who goes up, someone else goes down proportionately.)

Penalty for making less than the assigned number of tricks: On the next deal, player must give as many cards as points gained to the person who lost points. Each person receiving cards must give the penalized player the highest card in her hand. On the next deal (and all subsequent deals), the designated number of tricks for each player changes: 9 becomes 2, 5 becomes 9, and 2 becomes 5.

The game continues until one player reaches 0 and is the winner.

Learning skills: classification
                       number values
                       subtraction

Kajung

Ages: 4 - adult   **Players:** 2 - 4

This game is played by Indian children in the Yukon. "Kajung" means "rosehip".

Object of the game: To collect sets of three or more cards of the same denomination (three 2's or 3's, etc.) and runs of three or more cards in sequence of the same suit (e.g. 6, 7, 8), and, ultimately, to get three jacks.

First of all: Deal seven cards to each player and place deck face down on the table.

Play: Player to the dealer's left picks up the top card of the face-down pile and may add it to his hand or discard it. If he keeps it, he puts down another card from his hand. Each player in turn may take the top card from the discard pile, or the top card of the face-down deck, always discarding one card. At his turn, a player may meld (lay down face up in front of him) sets of three or more of a kind, or runs of three or more.

Special considerations: Eights are "wild". An 8 may be used to stand for any card in a set or a run. Whenever a player plays a 2 — either as a discard or a meld — other players must each take two cards from the decks. If a player melds a set of three 2's, each player must take six cards.

Play continues until one player gets three jacks ("Kajung"). If all the cards have gone through and no one has managed to get "Kajung", play continues with players discarding cards from their melds.

Learning skills: set-changing
                           numerical ordering
                           understanding special rules

Ace Frimé

Ages: 7 - adult   **Players:** 2 - 4

This game from France is one of the innumerable versions of rummy; in this one, the wild card changes from hand to hand.

Object of the game: To be first to get rid of all your cards.

Equipment: A deck of cards.

First of all: Deal seven cards to each player. Put the deck in the centre of the table and turn up the top card.

Play: Player to the dealer's left takes a card (the turned-up card if he wants it, otherwise the top card of the pack) and discards one. Play continues to the left. At a player's turn he may meld (lay down sets of cards face-up in front of him). Permissible melds are "three of a kind" (three or more cards of the same denomination) or runs of three or more cards of the same suit in sequence. Players (at their turn) may add to lay-outs on the table. When the fourth member of a set has been added, the four cards are turned over. As soon as a player puts down all his cards, the other players count the point value of cards in their hands. Each player's cards count *against* him.

Winner is the player with the lowest score after a designated number of hands.

Point value of cards: Ace through 10 = face value of cards (ace counts as 1); jack, queen, king = 10 points each; wild cards (the card designated as wild for each hand) = 15 points. Aces are wild in the first hand, 2's in the second, then 3's, and so on.

Learning skills: classification
numerical ordering
memory skills
set-changing
addition

Gimme

Ages: 7 - adult   **Players:** 5 or more

Object of the game: To be first to get rid of all the cards in your hand. Each game consists of seven hands, each of which begins in the same way.

Equipment: Two decks of cards with jokers (three decks for seven or more players) shuffled together.

First of all: Deal eleven cards to each player. Dealer puts the rest of the pack in the centre of the table and turns the top card face up. Player to the dealer's left may take that card. If he doesn't want it, any player who does may say, "Gimme". The one closest to the dealer gets it, but must take the top face-down card along with it.

Play: Each player in turns picks a card from the top of the deck and discards one. The player to his left may pick up the discard, but if he does not, other players may say "Gimme" and proceeds as above. A player is allowed only three "Gimme's" in any hand (that is, he may obtain a maximum of seventeen cards). Players, at their turn, may meld cards (lay sets face up in front of them) according to the following rules:

First hand: Two sets (a set consists of three to five cards of the same denomination). The two sets do not have to be laid down at the same time.

Second hand: One set, one run (a run consists of four to seven cards of the same suit in sequence).

Third hand: Two runs.

Fourth hand: Three sets.

Fifth hand: Two sets, one run.

Sixth hand: Two runs, one set.

Seventh hand: Three runs.

Jokers are wild (and may substitute for any card in a run or set).

A player, at his turn, may also put down cards that complement opponents' melds. For example, if there is a set of 7's on the table, a player can meld a 7 from his own hand, if an opponent has a run of 2, 3, 4, 5 of hearts, a player can meld an ace or 6 of hearts from his hand. A hand ends as soon as one player has no more cards. Other players total the value of all the cards left in their hands. These count against them. If, at any point in the game, one player has more than seventeen cards in his hands (that is, has taken more than three "Gimme's"), all of the cards in his hand count against him.

Point value of cards:

Jokers:	50
Aces:	25
All face cards:	10
All other cards:	5

Winner is the player with the lowest score after all seven hands have been played.

Learning skills: classification
  numerical ordering
  mental flexibility
  memory skills
  visual scanning
  addition
  counting by tens (the efficient way to score the
    face cards in your hand)

There are 15 920 024 220 different hands possible in gin rummy.

Back Alley Bridge

Ages: 7 - adult   **Players:** 2 - 4

Also known as Open Rummy, this is my favourite rummy game. It is thoroughly involving, fast moving, keeping players on their toes, always engaged in planning strategic moves.

Equipment: 2 decks of 52 cards shuffled together.

Object of the game: To lay out sets and runs in order to be first to get rid of all the cards.

Value of the cards: In play, Aces are low or high, so that permissible runs are Ace-two-three; Queen-King-Ace; or even King-Ace-2. In scoring, face cards are equal to 10 and other cards are equal to their face value. Ace = 1; two = 2, etc.

First of all: Deal 7 cards to each player and place the deck in the middle of the table.

Play: Each player, in turn, takes the top card off the deck and adds it to his hand. After picking a card, a player may "meld" — lay down cards in sets or runs face-up in the centre of the table. Permissible melds are 3 or more cards of the same denomination (but of different suits) or 3 same-suit cards in sequence (e.g. 2, 3, and 4 of spades). If a player cannot meld, play passes to the left.

At any turn a player may put down all possible melds, add to sets or runs on the table and rearrange sets and runs on the table to allow further play. Sets and runs can be taken apart and reassembled, as long as the result yields runs or sets of at least 3 cards. For example, if, on the table, there is a set of J, Q, K, A of diamonds and 8, 9, 10, J of spades and player's hand contains a J of hearts, player may remove the jack of diamonds and jack of spades from their respective runs and lay them down with the jack of hearts to make a set of jacks. Rearrangements may involve many different layouts where cards are ingeniously recombined to allow a play. When all possible moves have been made, player knocks on the table to indicate that next player may proceed. Play continues until one player has no more cards and is the winner of the hand.

124

Other players count up the value of cards remaining in their hands. Those points are credited to the score of the player who won the hand. At the end of an agreed number of hands, player with the highest score is the winner of the game.

Learning skills: ordering
classification
planning
mental flexibility
problem solving

Dammit

Ages: 7 - adult   **Players:** 2 - 4 or more

Another version of rummy, this one is from England.

Object of the game: To be first to get rid of all the cards in your hand.

Equipment: Two decks of cards with jokers. If there are five or more players, use three decks. Wild cards are jokers and 2's.

First of all: Deal eleven cards to each player. Put remainder of deck in the centre of the table and turn up the top card.

Special rules: A game consists of twelve or more hands. There are twelve "contracts" to be made in turn. Each player must make contract number 1 before he can make number 2, even if other players are on a second or third hand.

The contracts:
1. Two sets of three (a set is cards of the same denomination).
2. One set of three; one run of four (a run is cards of the same suit in sequence).
3. Two sets of four.
4. Two runs of four.
5. One set of four; one run of four.
6. Three sets of three.
7. One set of three; one run of seven.
8. Two sets of three; one run of four.
9. Two sets of five.
10. Two runs of five.
11. One run of eight.
12. One run of ten.

In any given set or run, wild cards cannot exceed the number of natural cards used.

Aces may be high (follow a king in a run) or low (precede a two).

Play: Player to the dealer's left may pick up the turned-up card, or may take the top card of the face-down pack. When he has taken a card, he discards one on the face-up pile. Next player may take either the top face-up card, or the top face-down card. He then discards one. Play proceeds to the left. At a player's turn, he may meld cards in keeping with his contract. He does not have to meld the entire contract at once. For example, if he has to make two sets, he can lay down one at a time.

After a contract is made, the other cards in the hand can be placed on contracts already on the board (e.g. a 2 on a set of 2's,; or a 10 of spades on a run of 6, 7, 8, 9 of spades).

When a player is out, other players' remaining cards count *against* them.

Scoring:

Jokers:	50
2's:	50
Aces:	25
9 to King:	10
3 to 8:	5

When the first person goes out after the twelfth contract has been made, the winner is the player with the lowest score — even if that player has not completed Contract 12.

Variation: Another version of rummy is called "Frustration". It is played out exactly like "Dammit" but twelve cards are dealt to each player, there are ten contracts to be made, the only wild cards are jokers, and the scoring is different.

The contracts:
1. Two sets of three.
2. One set of three; one run of three.
3. One run of four; one set of four.
4. Two runs of four.
5. One run of four; two sets of three.
6. One run of five; one set of three.
7. One run of seven; one set of three.
8. Two runs of four; one set of three.
9. Four sets of three.
10. Two runs of five.

Penalty for cards left in hand:
Joker:	20 points
Ace:	15 points
10-King	10 points
2-9	5 points

Learning skills: classification
numerical ordering
mental flexibility
memory skills
visual scanning
addition
counting by tens (the efficient way to score the face cards in your hand)

Seven Up

Ages: 4 - 12   **Players:** 2 - 4

Object of the game: To pick up cards ace through 7 and have them in sequence from left to right.

First of all: Deal each player seven face-down cards. Place the remaining cards in a pack face down in the middle of the table.

Play: Starting with the player at the dealer's left, players take turns taking a card from the centre pile. Player may use that card (if it is one of the desired cards) to replace one of his face-down cards, placing the new card face-up in the appropriate position. If the card that has been displaced can be used, player may place that card. If not, it is discarded face-up beside the centre face-down pile. At his turn, a player may take the top face-up card from the centre pile if he can use it. Otherwise, he draws from the face-down pile. Play continues until one player has ace through 7 faced up from left to right. That player is the winner.

Learning skills: numerical ordering

Cards in the arts: Movies have been made about card games. The Cincinnati Kid — about poker; A Big Hand for the Little Lady — about poker; The Flamingo Kid — about gin rummy. Trick 13 is a novel — a murder mystery set in the world of international tournament bridge. The Gin Game was a successful Broadway play. Menotti wrote an opera called The Game of Cards. In the collection of Her Majesty the Queen at Buckingham Palace is a painting by Pietr De Hooch — a 17th century Dutch painter, called The Card Game. A painting by Caravaggio, who lived between 1573 and 1610, called Il Baro shows two young boys playing cards for money. A bystander, looking over the shoulder of one of them, is signaling the other. The cards in the picture, with suit markings, but no numbers in the corner, look very much like my reproductions of Early American cards.

Durak

Ages: 7 - adult   **Players:** 2 preferred, may be played by 3.

This Russian game was sent to me by Dr. Meryl Green, skilled speech and language clinician in Boston, who knows a good card game when she sees it!

Object of the game: To get rid of all your cards once the deck is gone by "sending" or "hitting off" cards.

Equipment: 1 deck of cards. (I have a beautiful Russian deck that I like to use when I play this game. It adds to the cosmopolitan sense of playing a game from a faraway country.)

Value of cards: Cards increase in value from ace (low) to king (high).

First of all: Each player gets five cards. The next card is turned over and placed face up. The rest of the deck is placed on it so that it remains visible. The turned-up card determines trump.

Play: A player who has the 2 of trumps may, at his turn, exchange it for the turned-up trump card.

The first player (A) "sends" (lays on the table) one card, three cards (a "troika" — a pair and an outside card) or five cards (a "Pittyorka" — two pairs and an outside card) to the player (B) on the left. That player (B) "hits off" any of those cards by placing a higher card of the same suit or a trump on the card(s) sent. A card "hit off" is placed on the discard pile. Any cards not "hit off" are taken into player B's hand. Player B is not obligated to "hit off" cards. They may be added to player's hand and player may pass.

While there are cards in the stack, players must always have a minimum of five cards in hand.

If, after sending or "hitting off", there are fewer than five cards, player A draws from the deck to get the required number. If all cards sent to player B are not "hit off", that player may not send, and it is the next player's turn to send.

Once the deck is used up, the players try to have at least a troika (three) to send. This is not always possible. Play continues until one player plays his last card and is the winner.

Tips for good play: *Early in the game try to avoid sending trump or "hitting off" with trump. As the stack diminishes, trump can be used more brazenly. It is good to have a pair to send off at the end, especially one with a high trump.*

Learning skills: matching
relative value of numbers
counting
planning

Ninety-Nine

Ages: 8 - 12   **Players:** 3 - 6

Object of the game: This is an addition game. As cards are totalled, players try to avoid going beyond ninety-nine.

Equipment: A deck of cards.

Value of cards:

2-8:	face value
10:	minus 10
Jack:	12
Queen:	13
Ace:	1 or 11
King:	total automatically becomes 99
9:	0
4:	4, but reverses the order of playing

First of all: Three cards are dealt to each player and the pack is placed in the middle.

Play: Players play one card at a time in turn and pick up a card from the deck each time a card is laid down. As the first player plays his card, he says its value (say "2"). Second player adds on the value of her card (e.g. if she plays an 8 she says "10"). If a player plays a 4, the play proceeds in the opposite direction. If a player plays a 10, 10 is subtracted from the total. Game continues, with players trying to avoid going over 99. Player who goes over 99 is out of the game. Next player restarts count by playing a card, and play continues until only one player is left and is the winner.

Tips for good play: *Hang onto cards that can get you out of trouble, notably, 10, king, 9.*

Learning skills: mental addition and subtraction
memory development for detail
planning

Hit The Mark

Ages: 6 - 12   **Players:** 2 - 4

This game is named after Mark, the eight year old who taught it to me.

Object of the game: To accumulate low cards and to have the cards totalling the lowest value.

Value of cards: Cards equal their face value. Kings and queens each equal 10. Jacks = 0.

First of all: Deal five face-down cards to each player.

Play: Players take turns facing up cards from the centre pile. At his turn, each player may trade one of his face-down cards for a face-up card, immediately turning the new card face down in its place. The discarded card is added to the face-up pile and may be taken by an opponent if he wants to make a trade. At any point in the game, a player who thinks his cards have a low total value may "knock". By knocking on the table, he announces that he wants to face up his cards. All players then do so. The winner is the player whose cards have the lowest total value.

Tips for good play: *Players choose low-value cards and try to remember their position in the face-down array. This is essential so that they don't inadvertently trade them later in the game.*

Learning skills: visual memory for sequence
                      addition

Mark's Place

Ages: 7 - adult   **Players:** 4 - 5

One of the mathematical concepts for some children to grasp is that of place value. Yet, understanding it is basic to understanding regrouping; the ability to read and write multi-digit numbers depends on understanding place value. Using "Hit The Mark" as the inspiration, this game was developed to help children learn that each digit in a number has significance.

Object of the game: To get the highest value four-digit number, with a spade in the thousands place (on the left), a heart in the hundreds place (second from the left), a diamond in the tens place (third from the left), and a club in the ones place (on the right).

Equipment: Forty-card deck (face cards removed)

Value of cards: Spades: thousands (e.g. 5 of spades = 5 000)
Hearts: hundreds (e.g. 2 of hearts = 200)
Diamonds: tens (e.g. 7 of diamonds = 70)
Clubs: ones (e.g. 9 of clubs = 9)

First of all: Deal four face-down cards to each player. Place remainder of the deck in the centre of the table and turn up the top card.

Play: Player to the dealer's left may take the turned-up card and exchange it for one of his cards, facing up the card he does not want and placing it next to the deck to form a discard pile. If he does not want the face-up card, he takes the top card and can either exchange it for one of his cards or discard it. Play continues to the left, with each player having the option of taking the top face-up card on the discard pile or the top card of the pack.

As soon as a player thinks he has a card of each suit in the correct place and believes he has constructed the highest four-digit number of the group, then he can "knock". This is a demand that all players turn up their cards and compare them.

Scoring: If the player who knocked does have the highest value, he gets from each player the difference between his number and the highest value number that player can construct. If a player does not have the required suit in its place, then he considers that he has a zero in that place. For example, if a player's turned-up cards are 3 of hearts, 7 of hearts, 2 of diamonds, 6 of diamonds, then his number is 720; if he has 2 of spades, 5 of hearts, 4 of clubs, 8 of clubs, then his number is 2508.

If a player has a higher number than the player who knocked, he gets double the value of the differences between his number and the knocker's number and, from each of the other players, the difference between his number and theirs.

The first player whose score totals 10 000 is the winner.

Variation: The object of the game is to get the *lowest* possible number. To qualify, players must have one card in each suit in the correct spot. Include jacks in the deck; jack = 0. Needless to say, the jack of spades will be the most sought-after card.

Learning skills: an understanding of place value
　　　　　　　　the reading and constructing of multi-digit
　　　　　　　　　　numerals
　　　　　　　　directional awareness
　　　　　　　　visual memory for position in a horizontal array
　　　　　　　　subtraction involving multi-digit numbers

The deck of cards is sometimes likened to an almanac. The 52 cards remind us that there are 52 weeks in a year; 12 face cards suggest the 12 months of the year. Four suits suggest the four seasons of the year. And if we add up all the spots in a deck of cards — one for an Ace, two for a two, three for a three, and so on up to 11 for a Jack, twelve for a Queen, 13 for a King, and one more for a Joker, then we get the total of 365 — the number of days in a year.

X Marks The Spot

Ages: 6 - adult   **Players:** 2 - 4

This is another variation of "Hit The Mark" to develop an under-standing of place value and the ability to read and write multi-digit numbers.

Object of the game: To accumulate low cards and place them strategically so that, reading from left to right, cards will make the lowest five-digit number.

Equipment: A deck of cards.

Value of cards: Cards equal their face value. All face cards equal 0. In the five-card array, the furthest right is the units position, where a number equals itself; second from the right, it has ten times its value; third from the right, a hundred times; fourth from the right, a thousand times; the leftmost, ten thousand times.

First of all: Deal five face-down cards to each player. Place the remaining deck face down in the centre of the table.

Play: Players take turns facing up cards from the centre pile. At his turn, each player may trade one of his face-down cards (sight unseen) for a face-up card. The card taken is immediately placed face down in the position of the discarded card. The discarded card is placed on the face-up pile and may be taken by the next player if he wants to make a trade. At any point in the game, a player may "knock". This announces that he wants to face up his cards because he thinks his cards, reading from left to right, will make a five-digit numeral that is lower than any of his opponents'. All other players must then face up their cards. The winner is the player with the lowest five-digit number.

Scoring (optional): Each player subtracts the winning number from his number, and the result is his score. At the end of a predetermined number of rounds, winner is the player with the lowest score.

Tips for good play:
1. *Choose only cards of low denomination. Try to remember their*

position in the face-down array so that they won't be inadvertently traded later in the game.

2. *A face card (zero) should always be placed in the furthest left position that is possible. But remember that a face card placed on the very left would make a four-digit number, not a five-digit one.*

Variations:

1. For children just learning about place value and the reading and writing of multiple-digit numbers, deal only two cards and make the object of the game the lowest two-digit numeral. Then, when two-digit numbers are easily read and the child understands the difference between, for example, 23 and 32, play with three cards, then four, and finally work up to five cards.

2. Vary the object of the game. Aim to get the highest number, rather than the lowest.

Learning skills: an understanding of place value

the reading and constructing of multi-digit numerals

directional awareness

visual memory for position in a horizontal array

subtraction involving multi-digit numbers

A postage stamp with the Queen of Hearts on it was issued by Bermuda in January, 1975 to mark a world bridge championship.

The record for the youngest life master in bridge was set at a tournament in Montreal by Douglas Hsieh, age 11 years, 10 months. Douglas attributed his good intellectual ability to early card playing — particularly games of concentration when he was just a pre-schooler.

The number of possible 13 card bridge hands is 635 013 559 600.

Seven And A Half

Ages: 7 - adult   **Players:** 2 - 6

During lectures on card games, I often learn more than I teach. One class of language-disabilities specialists produced this game, offered by a Sicilian man as "Sette e Mezzo". A Venezualan woman recognized it as "Siete y Medio". Both played it with a forty-card deck, called Italian cards by one and Spanish cards by the other.

Object of the game: To get cards totalling as close to 7 ½ as possible without exceeding it.

Equipment: One deck of Italian or Spanish cards, or an ordinary deck with 8's, 9's, and 10's removed. Chips or counters.

Value of cards: All numerical cards are worth their face value (ace = 1, 2 = 2, etc.). Face cards = ½.

First of all: One player is selected as dealer. Players begin with an equal number of chips. These are used to bet against the dealer (that is,

to bet that one's own hand will be closer to 7½ than the dealer's).
Players may agree on a maximum bet.

The dealer gives each player, including himself, one face-down card.
Each player places a bet.

Play: Starting at the dealer's left, each player, in turn, decides whether
to "stand pat" or ask for another card. If, on taking another card, the
total of the cards is more than 7½, then that player's bet immediately
goes to the dealer. When a player decides to "stand pat" (take no more
cards), dealer moves on to the next player. When all the players have
drawn cards or overdrawn, dealer completes his own hand. Then all
cards are faced up.

Settlement: If dealer goes over 7½, he pays each player who has
not, the amount of the player's bet. If dealer has 7½ or less, then
players having the same number are tied and no chips change hands.
Players having less than the dealer pay their bet to the dealer. Players
closer to 7½ than the dealer win the amount of their bet from him.

Comments: *A perfect hand is 7 and a face card. Players may want to
stand pat at 5. Although most players will not draw more than two
cards, a player who initially gets several face cards may draw several
before there is a real danger of going over.*

Learning skills: addition
                        understanding the fractional value of ½
                        adding halves
                        calculating probabilities

Odds Or Evens

Ages: 5 - adult   **Players:** 2

Object of the game: To win all the cards.

First of all: The dealer holds up the cards one at a time, with the face of the card facing away from the player. The player must guess whether its value is odd or even (jacks = 11, queens = 12, kings = 13). If he guesses correctly he keeps the card in a face-down pile in front of him. If he guesses incorrectly, the dealer keeps it in his face-down pile. When all the cards have been handed out in this way, play begins.

Play: Dealer turns up his top card. Players note its colour and whether it is odd or even. This determines the winning card. Then they alternate turning up cards one at a time onto a central pile, until one of them turns up a winning card (black odd if the first card was black odd, etc.). Player takes in all the cards, placing them at the bottom of his stack, and turns up the top card on his pile. Again its colour and "oddness" or "evenness" are noted, and that determines the next winning card. Play continues in this way until one player gets all the cards.

Learning skills: understanding the mathematical concepts of "odd" and "even"
holding two variables in mind (colour and status as odd or even)

Add And Subtract

Ages: 7 - adult   **Players:** 2

Object of the game: To be the first to reach the desired total (70 for "add"; 30 for "subtract").

Value of cards: All cards have face value; jacks = 11, queens = 12, kings = 13.

First of all: Each player picks a card. Player with the higher card is "add". The other is "subtract". The entire deck is dealt out so that each player has half the deck in a face-down pile in front of him.

Play: The play begins with 50. Players take turns placing their top cards on a central pile and adding or subtracting its value from the cumulative total. For example:

Player	Card played	Player says
Add	7	57 (50 + 7)
Subtract	9	48 (57 − 9)
Add	3	51 (48 + 3)
Subtract	King	38 (51 − 13)

Scoring: If the total reaches 70, "add" is the winner. If it falls to 30, then "subtract" is the winner. If the cards run out before there is a winner, they are reshuffled and turned over.

Variations:
1. Start at 0, so that players use negative numbers. If the total reaches + 20, "add" wins; if it goes down to − 20, "subtract" is the winner.
2. Black numbers are positive. Red numbers are negative (an introduction to "in the red"). Players add to or subtract from the cumulative total, depending on the card they turn up. If players start at 50, first player to reach 75 or 25 is the winner.
3. Allow the use of a calculator for players who don't know number facts by heart and who can't make rapid mental calculations.

Learning skills: mental addition and subtraction
variations offer practice in using a calculator and practice in adding and subtracting negative numbers

Zero

Ages: 6 - 12   **Players:** 2

Object of the game: To win all the cards.

Equipment: A deck of cards.

Value of cards: Cards are equal to their face value, with jacks = 11, queens = 12, kings = 13. Black cards have positive value (+); red cards have negative value (−).

First of all: Deck is divided between the two players.

Play: Players play simultaneously, as in "War". Each turns up two cards at the same time. Player whose total value is closest to zero (0) takes in all four cards and puts them in a face-down pile. For example, if player A has a 4 of spades and Q of diamonds (+4 and −12 = −8) and player B has 4 of diamonds and king of clubs (−4 and +13 = +9), then player A is the winner. In the case of a tie (say player A has +2 and player B has −2), then each player turns up two more cards and totals them. Winner of that trick takes in all eight cards.

Learning skills: adding and subtracting negative numbers

Turnover Totals

Ages: 7 - adult   **Players:** 2

Object of the game: To get the highest point total or to be the first to reach 180.

Equipment: Deck of 36 cards: ace to 9 in each suit.

First of all: Shuffle cards. Deal them face down in a six-by-six matrix.

Play: First player turns over any card. Next player may turn over any card that touches it (top, bottom, left, right, or a diagonal). A running total is kept of the cards turned over. Each player keeps a personal tally and records the points whenever a card he turns over brings the total to 5 or any multiple of 5. Thus, if players A and B are playing, the score sheet below would represent the following moves.

Player	Card turned	Total
A	5	5
B	3	8
A	2	10
B	7	17
A	3	20
B	5	25
A	9	34
B	Ace	35

Score

A	**B**
5	25
10	35
20	

Learning skills: addition
five-times table

Jackblack

Not too many games provide an opportunity to practise subtraction, so I devised this game. Instead of trying to get cards totalling 21 as in Blackjack, players start with 21 and subtract card totals to get as close to 0 as possible.

Object of the game: To get cards totalling 0, or as close to 0 as possible, and to obtain a smaller total than the dealer without going below 0. The value of cards in a player's hand is subtracted from the original 21. Each player in the game plays and bets against the dealer.

Equipment: Deck of 52 cards; chips or tokens.

Value of cards: Jack, queen, and king each count as 10; 2 to 10 each counts its own face value; ace counts as 1 or 11.

First of all: Deal cards face up around to all the players. The first player receiving a jack becomes dealer and banker. Thereafter, deal passes to the left.

Players begin with an equal number of counters. These are used to bet against the dealer (i.e. to bet that one's own hand will be closer to 0 than the dealer's). A maximum bet is decided on by all players in advance. Before the deal, all players except the dealer place their bets (e.g. 1, 2, or 3 chips).

When the deal begins, each player has 21 points. The dealer gives each player, including himself, one card face up and one face down, one at a time, in rotation to the left.

Play: Each player checks his cards for "Jackblack", which consists of an ace and a ten-point card $(11 + 10)$. This gives a total of 0 $(21 - 21)$. If the dealer has Jackblack, each player, unless he has Jackblack himself, must give the dealer twice the amount of his bet. If a player has Jackblack and the dealer does not, he collects twice his bet from the dealer. If a player and the dealer both have Jackblacks, the dealer wins.

If the dealer does not have Jackblack, and after all players' Jackblacks have been paid off, the other players may "draw". Each player in turn

144

may ask for cards in order to bring his total as close to zero as possible. He asks for one card at a time (saying "hit me") until he is satisfied to "stand pat". Should he go below 0 (−1, −2, etc.), he immediately shows his cards and the dealer collects the bet. After all the players have drawn cards, the dealer then faces up both of his cards and draws if he wants to.

Settlement: If the dealer goes below 0, he pays each player who has not overdrawn the amount of his bet. When the dealer has 0 or more, and player is tied, the dealer wins. Players having more than the dealer pay their bet to him. Players closer to 0 than the dealer win the amount of their bet from him.

Learning skills: subtraction
calculating probabilities (that a card of a particular value might turn up)

For the first three or four hundred years of playing cards' history, there were no numbers or suit symbols in the corners. These were introduced in the 19th century so that poker players could squeeze their cards together and still read the hands. These decks were known as "squeezer" decks.

The number of possible 5 card poker hands is 2 598 960.

Caesars Hotel Casino in Atlantic City uses 500 decks of cards each day.

Three-Card Indian Poker

Ages: 7 - adult   **Players:** 3

Object of the game: To guess correctly the relative position of your numeral: high, low, or in the middle.

Equipment: A deck of cards; chips or tokens.

First of all: Remove the face cards and 10's. Each player is dealt three cards. After looking at them, players turn them over and mix them thoroughly so they have no idea of the relative positions of the cards. Then, without looking at the faces, they each raise the three cards and hold them to their foreheads, creating a three-digit numeral, visible to their opponents.

Play: Each player, after consulting his opponents' exposed cards, bets, putting in two chips, on the position of his own "numeral". Then all players look at their cards. The winner, the one who bet correctly, takes in all the chips. If two players bet correctly, they divide the pot. If all three are correct, or all three are wrong, the chips stay in to enrich the next pot.

Tips for good play: Player (P), knowing the three digits in his numeral, though not what place each occupies, may be able to calculate the probabilities of his relative position. If P's digits are, for example, 3, 7, and 8, and opponents' "numerals" are 452 and 921, P is twice as likely to be in the "middle" (with 7 or 8 in the 100's place) than "low" (with 3 in the 100's place). If P goes second or third, and other players have already made bets, P is in an even better position to make a guess that takes the opponents' reasoning into consideration.

Variation: Players do not see their own cards, but are told the total of their three cards. With only that information and the view of each of the opponents' three-digit numeral, players each guess whether their number is highest, lowest, or in the middle.

Learning skills: practice in reading three-digit numbers
place value
calculating probabilities
deductive reasoning

Thirty-One

Ages: 8 - adult   **Player:** any number

Object of the game: To have the hand with the highest value, thereby winning chips.

Equipment: A deck of cards; tokens or chips.

Value of cards: Only the following cards or combinations count: face cards = 10; aces = 11; three of a kind (any three cards of the same denomination) = 30.

First of all: Deal three cards to each player. Put the deck in the middle and turn over the top card. Players each bet two chips.

Play: Player to the dealer's right may take the face-up card or the top card of the deck. He then discards, facing up the card from his hand on the turned-up pile. Players, in turn, take a card (either the face-up card or the top card of the deck) and discard one.

At his turn, a player, if he thinks his hand is high, may "knock" (he knocks on the table to signal that he is challenging the other players). After the knock each of the players is allowed one turn. Then all expose their cards. If the knocker is not high he must pay 1 1/2 times his bet. The player with the highest hand takes in the chips. If a player gets 31 (two face cards and an ace), he wins automatically then and there, with no showdown.

Learning skills: addition
counting by tens
multiplication (1½ ×)

Multiplication Rummy

Ages: 8 - 16   **Players:** 2 - 4

Object of the game: To be first to lay down all your cards.

Equipment: One deck with face cards removed.

First of all: Players agree on what "table" they will be playing (e.g. the six-times table). As a variation, they may agree to play for four deals (complete run-throughs of the deck), starting with the six-times table and increasing it by one each deal. Deal seven cards to each player. Put the remaining deck in the middle and turn up the top card.

Play: The first player may take the exposed card or the top card of the deck. He must discard a card from his hand, placing it on top of the face-up card. Play continues in this fashion.

Players, at their turn, may lay down a card or combinations of two or three cards, using the numbers to form the digits of numerals that are multiples of the agreed-on number. If, for example, the game is built around the eight-times table, a player may lay down a 6 and a 4, as 64, because $8 \times 8 = 64$.

Tens may be used in two ways: a 10 can be laid out with another card placed across it to indicate that the 10 is being multipled by that

number; thus, if we were playing "eights" a 10 could be played with a 4 across it to stand for 40 ($5 \times 8 = 40$).

Tens can also be used to represent the digit 10. For example, in playing "nines", a player might lay down a 10 and an 8 as 108, because $12 \times 9 = 108$.

Play continues until one player gets rid of all the cards and is the winner of that deal.

Scoring: To calculate their points, losers count the cards remaining in their hands and multiply the number by the key number for that deal (e.g. 8 if they're playing "eights").

Overall winner is the player with the lowest number of points at the end of four deals.

Suggestions: For children who do not know their tables, have the tables available, or provide the player who needs it with a calculator. The repetition provided by playing will help make the multiplication facts automatic.

Learning skills: rehearsal of multiplication facts

Three-Card Brag

Object of the game: To have the "highest" hand.

Equipment: Deck of cards; chips or tokens.

Value of cards: Card values, in descending order, are A, K, Q, J, 10, through 2. Hand values in ascending order:
— pairs (two cards of the same denomination)
— three of a kind (three cards of the same denomination)
— run (three cards in ascending order, regardless of suit, e.g. 2 of spades, 3 of hearts, 4 of diamonds)
— flush (any three cards of the same suit)
— running flush (three cards in sequence of the same suit)

If two players have the same kind of hand, the highest card values win.

First of all: Deal three face-down cards to each player. All players "ante" — put a chip in the pot to indicate they are in the game.

Play: Players in turn look at cards and either "fold" (go out of the game) or place a chip in the pot, indicating that they bet their hand is high. When all players have placed their bets, hands are turned over and the highest hand wins. If there are no pairs, runs, flushes, etc., then the hand with the highest card wins.

Learning skills: matching
ordering
classifying

Acey-Deucey

Ages: 6 - adult   **Players:** any number

Object of the game: To be first to get Acey-Deucey — an ace and two face cards of the same suit.

First of all: Deal three cards to each person. Place pack face down in centre and turn up the top card.

Play: Player to the dealer's left may take the exposed card, or take the top card of the pack. He then discards one card face up, leaving three cards in his hand. Each subsequent player may pick up the top card of the face up pile or the top card of the face down pile, discarding one of his cards immediately.

First player to reach the objective of two face cards and an ace of the same suit is the winner.

Strategies: Watch discards carefully. If, for example, the ace of the suit you are saving gets discarded and you do not have access to it, you will have to change the suit you are trying to collect. Be careful, too, not to give player to your left a card he may need to complete his Acey-Deucey.

Learning skills: classifying
memory for key cards
planning
revising strategies

Hold 'Em

Ages: 8 - adult   **Players:** 2 - 6

This game originated in Texas and is played by serious gamblers at the Poker World Series in Las Vegas. Though adults generally associate poker and all its variants with the dissolute world of the casino, with fortunes and time squandered, poker is really a lovely game, which can help to develop both intellectual and social skills. Kids can have a wonderful time playing it and can learn a lot in the process.

Poker is a gambling game, and betting is essential to the play, so there have to be stakes. Chips or tokens should be used that can be exchanged for something of real value. In a family, it can be privileges; for example, ten red chips can be cashed in for the right not to make the bed that day; in a classroom, for a night with no homework.

In poker, actually known as "bluff" in French, bluffing is very much part of the action. Bluffing — pretending to have a good hand, thereby scaring other players out of the hand — is used to win games. It is also used to obtain information and to mislead other players. A player may bluff — continue to bet on a hand he knows he will lose — so that he can see his opponent's cards. This enables him to learn something about the other player's betting and bluffing behaviour. Or he may bet on an obviously poor hand just to get the other players to misjudge his playing style. So, part of poker is learning the skill of reading your opponents' behaviour and keeping them guessing about yours. This means developing the "poker face" — no grinning when you peek at your cards and see you have two aces. A poker game is a good vehicle for a fidgety, restless adolescent to practise holding down his tendency to drum his fingers on the table or shuffle his feet, or whistle when he is under tension. Similarly, it is the ideal situation for learning to look for cues in other people's behaviour. Some adolescents with learning disabilities are socially inept because they can't read the subtleties of behaviour that signal that someone is worried or angry or depressed. Watching fellow poker players for tell-tale signs is a good way to learn the cues.

Object of the game: To get the highest valued five-card hand, using any of seven cards: two "hole" cards (face-down cards dealt to each player) and five communal cards.

Equipment: A deck of cards; chips or tokens.

Value of cards: The hands, from highest to lowest:
— straight flush (five same-suit cards in sequence)
— four of a kind (four cards of the same denomination)
— full house (a pair and three of a kind)
— flush (five cards of the same suit)
— straight (five cards in sequence, regardless of suit)
— three of a kind
— two pairs
— one pair
— if none of the above, the hand with the highest card.
If two or more players have pairs, etc., then the higher denominations are higher valued.

First of all: Players draw a card to determine the dealer. High card deals the first hand. Deal passes to the left. For authentic casino play, dealer does not play the hand, and an indicator, called the "button", is placed in front of each player in turn to announce that he is the dealer for that hand. A hockey puck makes a good button. Each player "antes" (bets on an agreed-on amount, say, one chip). Then the dealer deals each player two face-down cards.

Play: Player to the dealer's left must bet (that is, put in one or more chips). The other players, in turn, must either "see" the bet (that is, put in an amount equal to the bet in order to stay in the game); "raise" the bet (in which case all players must equal that bet to stay in) or "fold" — go out of the hand, thereby forfeiting any money already bet.
Dealer than deals three more cards face-up on the table. These are communal cards and are called the "flop". Players bet again, this time calculating their strength on the basis of five cards. At this betting round players may "check", that is, not bet any more chips but stay in the game. Of course, if one player bets, the others must at least "see" him to stay in the game. Then a fourth communal card is dealt, followed by a round of betting. Finally, dealer deals a fifth card. Players bet one more time (or fold) and then there is the show-down. The winner, the player with the highest valued hand, takes the chips.

Learning skills: learning to read facial cues and body language
practising self-control
calculating probabilities
remembering the relative value of poker hands

In Between

Ages: 5 - adult   **Players:** any number

Object of the game: To bet correctly that the third card dealt will be in between the first two in numerical value.

Equipment: A deck of cards; chips or tokens.

First of all: One player is designated dealer and does not get cards. Players take turns as dealer. Two cards are dealt to each player face up.

Play: A player may "fold" (withdraw from betting) or bet. He bets that the number of the next card dealt will be *in between* the two numbers on the cards already faced up. The number of chips bet will reflect his confidence in his bet. (The farther apart the two cards are in value, the greater the probability of getting a card that is in between.) If a player has bet correctly, dealer must pay him the amount of his bet. Lost bets are collected by the dealer.

Learning skills: understanding concepts of "in between",
                    "higher", "lower"
             calculating probabilities

Guts

Ages: 7 - adult   **Players:** 2 or more

Object of the game: To have any pair or the best combinations possible.

Equipment: Deck of cards; chips or tokens.

Value of cards: Pairs are most valuable, ranking in value from aces (high) down to 2's (low). When there are no pairs, the most valuable combinations are ace plus a face card, regardless of suit. Rank order is as follows (from highest to lowest):

> AK
> AQ
> AJ
> KQ
> KJ
> QJ

First of all: Deal three cards to each player.

Play: Player bets after looking at cards. A bet consists of putting down a chip and signifies that the player believes he has the best hand. Player has the option of discarding any card and asking for one more. Players in turn can "fold" (put down their cards and withdraw from the game) or play and bet.

When all players have bet and have had the option of drawing a new card, they bet again to "show". That is, those who wish to remain in the game bet one more time, turn up their cards, and the winning hand takes in the money.

Learning skills: memory (for key combinations)
learning arbitrary orders
calculating probabilities

Black Maria

Ages: 7 - adult   **Players:** best for 3

"Black Maria" is a very old game, dating back several centuries. It is relatively new to me, however. As a child I played "Hearts", the game which must have evolved from "Black Maria".

Object of the game: To avoid taking tricks that contain key cards.

Equipment: Deck of cards with the 2 of diamonds removed.

Rank of cards: Ace high, down to 2 low.

Value of cards: These cards score against the player who takes them in:

each heart = 1
Ace of spades = 7
King of spades = 10
Queen of spades = 13

First of all: Deal seventeen cards to each player. Before play begins, each player takes three cards from her hand — the cards she is most happy to get rid of — and passes them, face down, to the player on her right. Players then add the cards they have received to their hands.

Play: Player to the dealer's left leads any card. Players must follow suit. Highest card of suit led takes in the trick, and the player who takes the trick leads to the next trick. If a player cannot follow suit, any card may be discarded. That, of course, is the player's chance to stick her opponents with cards that will count against them.

Scoring: Players' scores are the total of the cards that count against them. Play continues until one player reaches 100 (and is the loser). Player with the lowest score is the winner.

Learning skills: categorizing and counting
judging relative rank of numbers
considering several factors at once
mental flexibility
addition
reasoning
memory
calculating probabilities
developing strategies

One Hundred And Fifty

Ages: 8 - adult   **Players:** 2

Object of the game: To gain 150 points by taking in tricks and cards with point values.

Equipment: 32-card deck (plus two jokers, optional). Remove 2's, 3's, 4's, 5's, and 6's from an ordinary deck.

First of all: Deal each player sixteen cards in two rows of four face-down cards, with one face-up card on each. If two jokers have been used, then deal the two remaining cards face down as a "kitty". The non-dealer may exchange any two cards in his hand for the kitty without looking at it first. If he doesn't want it, dealer may exchange two cards for it.

Value of cards: cards = face value; ace is high; jokers are highest trump cards. Players designate one as the smaller, the other the larger.

Point value: 10's = 10
Kings = 25
Last hand taken = 10

Bidding: First player bids his estimate of the number of points he will take in if he becomes the one to name trump. (Total points possible: four kings at 25 each; four tens at 10 each, and last hand for 10 points = 150). Bidding starts at 60. Players take turns bidding until one is unwilling to top opponent's bid. Highest bidder names trump.

Play: Highest bidder leads first card. Players must follow suit. If they cannot, they may trump. Trump card outranks all non-trumps. Highest card takes in trick, and player who takes trick plays a card. As top cards are played, underneath card is faced up.

If player makes his bid he is credited with his points. If he fails to make bid, he goes "in the hole" by the total amount of his bid. Thus, a player who bids 70 but only makes 60 is 70 in the hole, that is, − 70. Opponent is credited with points taken in, in this case 90. First player to reach 150 is the winner.

Learning skills: categorizing
counting
estimating
calculating probabilities
judging relative value of numbers
developing strategies
addition (including negative numbers)

The Best of Cards Catalog, available from U.S. Games Systems, Inc., 38 East 32nd Street, New York, N.Y. 10016, features hundreds of decks of cards — novelty decks, decks from around the world, reproductions of antique playing cards, historical decks, Tarot cards and other fortune telling decks, as well as books on playing cards.

Cards were used educationally back in the 16th century. Decks were especially developed to teach philosophy, heraldry, geography, history, grammar, arithmetic, and spelling.

"Rule Number One: Always try to see your opponent's cards." — From a handbook on "Scopa", a common Italian card game.

Last night I held a hand in mine,
So fair and pink and kind,
I swear I never held before
A fairer hand in mine.
I pressed it to my burning lips,
Kissed all five pink white parts
Of that dear hand I held last night —
The Royal Flush of Hearts.

Sixty-Three

Ages: 7 - adult   **Players:** 2 teams of 2

Object of the game: To be the first team to get to 200.

Equipment: Deck of fifty-two cards plus one joker.

First of all: Deal nine cards to each player. Put the rest of the pack aside. Partners face each other.

Value of cards: In play, cards have their face value with ace high and joker the low card, below a 2. For scoring purposes the following point value is used for trump cards taken in:

   Ace = 1
   King = 25
   Jack = 1
   Ten = 1
   Nine = 9
   Five = 5; opposite five = 5 (The "opposite five" is the 5 of the same colour as the trump cards, e.g. if diamonds are trump, then the opposite 5 is the 5 of hearts.)
   Two = 1
   Joker = 15
Total point value is 63.

Play: After looking at their cards, players bid for the privilege of naming trump. Player to the dealer's left begins the bidding. The bid is the number of points player estimates that he can make if he names trump. Bids are usually multiples of 5, but after 60 players can go as high as 63. The bid goes around until all pass except one player. When the bid is made, trump is named and players discard all cards except trump.

The successful bidder picks up the pack and deals cards to players so that they will have a total of 6. Then he plays a card which must be a trump. Players must follow suit if they can. Player who takes in the trick may lead in the following tricks. Play continues until the hand is finished. Partners then count up their points. If the player has not made his bid (counting both his and his partner's points), the amount of his bid is subtracted from his score. Opponents are credited with their own points.

Cards are redealt and game continues until one pair reaches 200 points and is the winning team.

Tips for good play:
1. *Don't bid 63 unless you have the King, Jack, and ten of trump.*
2. *Try to work in cooperation with your partner, taking in valuable cards whenever possible. If your partner plays a valuable card, say a 5, and you can take it, do so.*

Learning skills: calculating probabilities
estimating the value of a hand
working in cooperation with a partner
flexibility — distinguishing between a card's value
in play and its value in scoring
keeping track of many variables

Japanese cards are unusually beautiful. They consist of 48 cards, each depicting a flower. The flowers group into sets of four, each set representing a month. The cards are usually very small, with stencilled or enamelled designs and black, glazed cardboard backs.

Cards were played on the ships of Christopher Columbus and other Spanish explorers. They taught the game to the natives in Central America and North America. Indians made cards of animal hides and painted them in the Spanish way.

Bezique

Ages: 8 - adult   **Players:** 2

Object of the game: To earn points by taking in tricks that contain valuable cards or by laying down valuable combinations.

Equipment: Two decks of cards with the 2's, 3's, 4's, 5's, and 6's removed.

First of all: Deal eight cards to each player, dealing three at a time, then two, then three. Place deck in the centre of the table. Remove the top card and place it face up, so it shows, at the bottom of the stack. This determines trump.

Play: First player plays any card. Players do not have to follow suit except for the last eight tricks of the game. Highest card of suit led, or highest trump, takes in trick. After a trick has been taken, each player picks a card from the stack so that there are always eight cards in a hand.

Players may lay down certain cards (see "Points") from their hand face up in front of them. Even after they are placed face-up in front of a

player, these cards are still part of the hand and are available for play. When the stack gets down to four cards (three face down, one face up), the winner of the trick gets one face-down card and the face-up trump card. The other player gets the remaining face-down two.

Play continues until one player gets 1500 points and is the winner (about six times through the double deck).

Points: Each ace and ten that are taken in tricks count 10 points.

Point scoring combinations for lay-outs:
    Queen of spades and Jack of diamonds = 40 (Bezique)
If, while these are face up, a second identical Queen-Jack pair is placed with them, it's a Double Bezique = 400.

four aces	80
four kings	60
four queens	40
four jacks	30
four 10's	20
10, J, Q, K, A of same suit	80

Learning skills: categorizing
judging relative value of numbers
memory
planning
counting
addition

All Fours

Ages: 8 - adult   **Players:** 2 - 4

Object of the game: To get the highest number of points by taking in tricks, capturing key cards, and holding key cards.

Value of cards:
Cards kicked (top card turned over by first player):
ace:	1 point
6:	2 points
jack:	3 points

Cards played:
highest trump:	1 point
lowest trump:	1 point
jack of trump:	1 point (unless he has been "hung")
any card that hangs	
the jack of trump:	3 points

Cards taken in:
ace:	4 points
king:	3 points
queen:	2 points
10:	10 points

Player with highest total gets "game".

First of all: Dealer deals six cards to each player. First player to the dealer's left "kicks" (turns over) top card. This determines trump. If the first player objects to that trump, three more cards are dealt and player kicks again.

Play: First player may play any card. Players must follow suit or may trump (even if able to follow suit). The highest card played in a suit (or the highest trump) takes in the trick. Winner leads to the next trick. Play continues until all the cards have been played.

If a jack of trumps is played, player gets a point unless it is "hung" by the opponent. Jack is "hung" when opponent plays a higher card — queen, king, or ace.

Scoring: When all six cards have been played, players count 1 for each trick; 1 for Game (i.e. for having the highest number of points taken in tricks) (ace = 4 points, king = 3, queen = 2, 10 = 10); and then they add the points earned for a valuable kicked card, for having held highest card, highest trump, lowest trump, jack of trump (unless hung), or for having a card that hung the jack of trumps.

Learning Skills: memory development
mental flexibility
planning
developing strategies
addition

Scopa

Ages: 6 - adult   **Players:** 2 or 2 teams of 2

This game is well-known to Italian children, and means "broom".

Object of the game: To get the most points. The first player to get cards totalling 11 is the winner.

Equipment: An Italian deck of cards. If you don't have Italian cards, remove 8's, 9's, and 10's from an ordinary deck of 52.

Value of cards: All number cards equal their face value; jacks = 8, queens = 9, kings = 10.

First of all: Dealer deals four cards to each player, and four face-up cards on the table.

Play: Players take turns playing a card from their hand. A card may be used as a match to take in a card of the same denomination; or it can take in more than one card if the card to be played equals the total of two or more cards on the table.

For example, a 6 and a 2 on the table may be taken by a jack, a 3 and ace by a 4. When players take in cards, they keep them face down in a pile in front of them.

If a player manages, at any point, to pick up the last card on the table, that is a "Scopa". That card is turned up in the pile of accumulated cards, to be scored separately when the players tally their points.
After the four cards have been played out, the dealer deals four more to each player. The play continues until all cards have been dealt out. Then players tally their points.

Each turned-up card ("Scopa")	1 point
Each 7	1 point
King of diamonds	1 point
Most cards	1 point
Most diamonds	1 point

Learning skills: matching
addition
keeping track of several variables

Briscola

Ages: 6 - adult   **Players:** 2

Object of the game: To take in cards, thereby earning points.

Equipment: If you have an Italian deck, use it. If not, remove the 8's, 9's, and 10's and play with forty cards.

Value of cards: Cards have their denominational value.

Point value: Only the following cards earn points:

Ace:	11
3:	10
K:	4
Q:	3
J:	2

First of all: Deal three cards to each player, and turn up the top card of the deck. This determines the trump suit — that is, the suit with the most value.

Play: First player leads any card. Second player may follow suit but does not have to. If the second player follows suit, the highest card takes it in. If he doesn't follow suit and doesn't play a trump card, then the first player takes the cards in. The player who takes in the cards leads the next suit and the play continues. Player picks up a card after each play.

When all cards have been played, players tally their points. There are 120 points in the deck. The winner of the hand must have more than 60.

Winner of the game is the winner of two out of three hands.

Learning skills: classifying
understanding the relative value of numbers
addition
remembering key cards

Sentence Rummy

Ages: 6 - adult   **Players:** 2 - 4

Object of the game: To lay out cards in "sentences". In this game, cards have an alphabetical value, rather than a numerical one. Each card stands for the first letter of its name, i.e. ace = A, king = K, queen = Q, jack = J, two = T, three = T, four = F, etc.

First of all: Deal seven cards to each player, leaving the pack in the middle. Turn up the top card of the pack.

Play: As in other rummies, a player, at his turn, may take the turned-up card or the top card of the pack, and must discard a card. At his turn, he may lay out a set of at least four cards, composing a sentence of the same number of words, each beginning with one of the card letters. For example, player lays down ace, king, four, and seven, saying "A knife fell softly." Players may, at their turn, add to their own or another player's layout with a card that can be inserted in or added to the sentence. For example, a player may place a 6 between the ace and the king in the above layout, saying "A silver knife fell softly."

For each card laid down, player must pick a card from the pack so that there are always seven cards in a hand.

Play continues until the deck is used up and the last layouts have been made.

Scoring: Layouts are scored as soon as they are made and the points recorded. A five-card sentence is worth 5 points. Adding a single card to make a six-card sentence earns that player 6 points.

Winner is the player with the highest score.

Sample layouts and accompanying sentences:

4 Q 2 6 7:   Father quit the Secret Service.
8 3 7 5 6:   Eat the soup for supper.

Learning skills: vocabulary
verbal fluency
grammatical awareness
phonic awareness

Three-In-A-Row For Four

Ages: 4 - adult   **Players:** 4

Object of the game: To get three cards of one suit in a row horizontally, vertically, or diagonally.

First of all: Each player takes all of the cards in one suit.

Play: First player places a card (face up) on the table. Each player in turn must place a card so that it is touching (on the sides, top, bottom, or corners) a card already played. The first person to get three of his cards in a row is the winner.

Learning skills: planning ahead
    developing strategies
    sensitivity to two-dimensional spatial relations and
        the vocabulary to represent them: side, top,
        bottom, corner, vertical, horizontal, diagonal

Four In A Row

Ages: 5 - adult   **Players:** 2

Object of the game: To get four cards of the same suit in a row. Row may be vertical, horizontal, or diagonal.

First of all: One player takes all of the cards in a red suit, the other all of the cards in a black suit.

Play: First player (red) puts one card on the table. The other player can play a card so that it is touching the first card on any side or on a corner. Play continues, with players alternating, playing cards that touch cards already played. Player who gets four of his cards in a row is the winner.

Learning skills: careful planning
    the need to watch for opportunities to make
        strategic plays and at the same time to block
        the opponent's play

Alliteration

Ages: 6 - 12   **Players:** 2 - 8

Object of the game: To win all the cards.

First of all: Deal six cards to each player. Players place cards in face-down pile in front of them.

Play: Player to the dealer's left begins by saying, "I went to the department store and bought . . ." As soon as he has said "bought", he turns over his top card to a central pile and continues by saying the number of the turned-up card and a noun that begins with the same letter as the number of the card. For example, for a two he might say, "two tangerines"; for a four, "four firecrackers". For an ace, instead of

"one", player uses "an" and so might say, "an avocado". For face cards, no number is used, simply the first letter of the card. So, for a jack, player might say "a jellybean"; for a queen, "a quince", and for a king, "a kite". If player continues his sentence correctly without hesitating, he takes in the card. If not, he leaves it there, to be taken in by the next player to win the top card.

Play continues this way until all the cards are played. The player with the most cards wins. If there is no winner, cards are dealt again. This time, players must precede the noun with an adjective (e.g. "five fine forks"; "ten tiny turnips"; "a queer quilt"; etc.).

Variations: To encourage further vocabulary building, vary the carrier sentence: "I went to the zoo and saw . . ."; "I went to the toy store and bought . . ."

To elicit verbs instead of nouns, use this sentence: "My grandmother told me never to . . ." This can be made more difficult by requiring players to add two alliterative words — a verb and an adverb, or a verb and a noun. Children will begin to see the differences between verbs that are transitive (requiring an object) and those that are intransitive. Some examples of sentences produced in this variation of the game follow:

My grandmother told me never to . . .
    act angry
    tease turtles
    throw tantrums
    faint foolishly
    fall fast
    swallow sardines
    speak sarcastically
    eat eels
    nibble nuts
    terrify tarantulas
    joke jovially
    quit quoting
    kick kittens

Learning skills: practice in phonics (initial sounds of words)
    verbal fluency
    understanding of sentence structure and parts of
      speech
    sensitivity to alliteration

Coffee Pot

Ages: 6 - adult   **Players:** 2

Object of the game: To learn a concept — "Coffee Pot" — in as few trials as possible.

First of all: Each player picks a card. The player with the highest card is the "waiter". The other player is the "customer". The waiter decides on the definition of a "coffee pot". This is a set of three cards with certain characteristics, e.g. all even, all of the same colour, all under five.

Play: Waiter puts together several examples of "coffee pots" and "non-coffee pots" and shows them to the customer one at a time. Customer decides when he thinks he knows the definition, i.e., what makes a "coffee pot". Waiter then shows new examples and non-examples and customer has to classify each as "coffee pot" or "non-coffee pot." The game continues until customer has classified ten consecutive sets correctly. Then players switch roles.

Scoring: Players keep track of number of examples customer requires before he gets ten consecutive sets. This includes introductory examples as well as all correct and incorrect guesses that precede ten consecutive classifications. This number becomes customer's score. At the end of an agreed number of rounds, player with the lowest score is the winner.

Sample game:

4	5	4	This is a coffee pot.
4	5	6	This is not a coffee pot.
5	5	4	This is a coffee pot.
2	3	10	This is a coffee pot.
2	2	3	This is a coffee pot.
2	2	4	This is not a coffee pot.
6	7	7	This is a coffee pot.

Customer announces readiness to be tested.
Waiter presents:

| A | A | A | Customer says, "not a coffee pot". |
| | | | Waiter says, "wrong". |

172

Customer asks for one more example.

10   10   3   This is a coffee pot.

Customer is ready again.

				Customer's guesses	Waiter's responses
1.	2	3	10	Coffee pot	Right
2.	4	4	5	Coffee pot	Right
3.	4	4	2	No coffee pot	Right
4.	8	8	8	Coffee pot	Right
5.	A	A	4	No coffee pot	Right
6.	6	6	7	Coffee pot	Right
7.	9	9	A	No coffee pot	Right
8.	9	10	2	Coffee pot	Wrong
9.	5	5	4	Coffee pot	Right
10.	9	9	9	Coffee pot	Right

For readers who may not have figured it out, the definition of a "coffee pot" in this particular round was "a set with all numbers starting with the same letter".

Learning skills: deductive reasoning
classification
problem solving

Index